4·18
9-19 41

Global
Warming

Shasta Gaughen, *Book Editor*

Bruce Glassman, *Vice President*
Bonnie Szumski, *Publisher*
Helen Cothran, *Managing Editor*
David Haugen, *Series Editor*

Contemporary Issues
Companion

GREENHAVEN PRESS
An imprint of Thomson Gale, a part of The Thomson Corporation

THOMSON
━━━━★━━━━ ™
GALE

Detroit • New York • San Francisco • San Diego • New Haven, Conn.
Waterville, Maine • London • Munich

For more information, contact
Greenhaven Press
27500 Drake Rd.
Farmington Hills, MI 48331-3535
Or you can visit our Internet site at http://www.gale.com

LIBRARY OF CONGRESS CATALOGING-IN-PUBLICATION DATA

Global warming / Shasta Gaughen, book editor.
    p. cm. — (Contemporary issues companion)
    Includes bibliographical references and index.
    ISBN 0-7377-2651-2 (lib. : alk. paper) — ISBN 0-7377-2652-0 (pbk. : alk. paper)
    1. Global warming. I. Gaughen, Shasta. II. Series.
    QC981.8.G56.G545 2005
    363.738'74—dc22   2004049294

Printed in the United States of America

CONTENTS

FOREWORD

In the news, on the streets, and in neighborhoods, individuals are confronted with a variety of social problems. Such problems may affect people directly: A young woman may struggle with depression, suspect a friend of having bulimia, or watch a loved one battle cancer. And even the issues that do not directly affect her private life—such as religious cults, domestic violence, or legalized gambling—still impact the larger society in which she lives. Discovering and analyzing the complexities of issues that encompass communal and societal realms as well as the world of personal experience is a valuable educational goal in the modern world.

Effectively addressing social problems requires familiarity with a constantly changing stream of data. Becoming well informed about today's controversies is an intricate process that often involves reading myriad primary and secondary sources, analyzing political debates, weighing various experts' opinions—even listening to firsthand accounts of those directly affected by the issue. For students and general observers, this can be a daunting task because of the sheer volume of information available in books, periodicals, on the evening news, and on the Internet. Researching the consequences of legalized gambling, for example, might entail sifting through congressional testimony on gambling's societal effects, examining private studies on Indian gaming, perusing numerous websites devoted to Internet betting, and reading essays written by lottery winners as well as interviews with recovering compulsive gamblers. Obtaining valuable information can be time-consuming—since it often requires researchers to pore over numerous documents and commentaries before discovering a source relevant to their particular investigation.

Greenhaven's Contemporary Issues Companion series seeks to assist this process of research by providing readers with useful and pertinent information about today's complex issues. Each volume in this anthology series focuses on a topic of current interest, presenting informative and thought-provoking selections written from a wide variety of viewpoints. The readings selected by the editors include such diverse sources as personal accounts and case studies, pertinent factual and statistical articles, and relevant commentaries and overviews. This diversity of sources and views, found in every Contemporary Issues Companion, offers readers a broad perspective in one convenient volume.

In addition, each title in the Contemporary Issues Companion series is designed especially for young adults. The selections included in every volume are chosen for their accessibility and are expertly edited in consideration of both the reading and comprehension levels of the audience. The structure of the anthologies also enhances accessibility. An introductory essay places each issue in context and provides helpful facts such as historical background or current statistics and legislation that pertain to the topic. The chapters that follow organize the material and focus on specific aspects of the book's topic. Every essay is introduced by a brief summary of its main points and biographical information about the author. These summaries aid in comprehension and can also serve to direct readers to material of immediate interest and need. Finally, a comprehensive index allows readers to efficiently scan and locate content.

The Contemporary Issues Companion series is an ideal launching point for research on a particular topic. Each anthology in the series is composed of readings taken from an extensive gamut of resources, including periodicals, newspapers, books, government documents, the publications of private and public organizations, and Internet websites. In these volumes, readers will find factual support suitable for use in reports, debates, speeches, and research papers. The anthologies also facilitate further research, featuring a book and periodical bibliography and a list of organizations to contact for additional information.

A perfect resource for both students and the general reader, Greenhaven's Contemporary Issues Companion series is sure to be a valued source of current, readable information on social problems that interest young adults. It is the editors' hope that readers will find the Contemporary Issues Companion series useful as a starting point to formulate their own opinions about and answers to the complex issues of the present day.

Introduction

In January 2001 the Intergovernmental Panel on Climate Change (IPCC), a group of scientific experts assembled by the United Nations, released a frightening report on the potential consequences of the climate phenomenon known as global warming. The panel found that the 1990s had been the warmest decade on record and predicted that temperatures will rise anywhere from 2.5 to 10.4 degrees around the world over the next century, causing changes to global weather patterns. Indeed, unusual and frequently destructive weather had been occurring around the globe: twenty-seven inches of rain in one day in Hilo, Hawaii; an unheard-of thunderstorm in Barrow, Alaska; a huge ice storm in Atlanta, Georgia; massive floods in Europe; and an unprecedented high temperature of eighty-two degrees Fahrenheit in Iqaluit, a town in the Canadian Arctic. If these new weather patterns continue, the panel warned, the whole world could be facing a devastating environmental catastrophe resulting in massive floods, rising seas that wipe out coastal communities, rampant epidemics, millions of people left homeless, plant and animal extinctions on an unprecedented scale, and widespread starvation.

What Causes Global Warming?

Approximately two-thirds of the energy earth receives from the sun is absorbed by land masses and oceans and is then released into the atmosphere as warm, long-wave radiation. The atmosphere of earth is full of so-called greenhouse gases such as water vapor, carbon dioxide, ozone, methane, and nitrous oxide that act like a blanket, trapping some of the heat radiating from the land and oceans and preventing too much energy from escaping into space. The gas blanket works in much the same way as the glass panels of a greenhouse, serving to trap energy and keep temperatures at a steady level. The trapped heat keeps earth at a comfortable average temperature of about sixty-three degrees Fahrenheit. This process is known as the greenhouse effect.

Without the protection of the greenhouse gas blanket, life on earth would be difficult or impossible. To illustrate the importance of the greenhouse effect, climate expert Mark Maslin compares earth with Mars and Venus. The atmosphere on Mars does not contain enough carbon dioxide to trap much solar energy, causing the average surface temperature of the planet to stay about 122 degrees Fahrenheit. Venus, on the other hand, has a much thicker atmosphere than earth, consisting of approximately 96 percent carbon dioxide. This massive greenhouse blanket results in a surface temperature of 860 degrees Fahrenheit. Maslin's example reveals that the precise combination of greenhouse gases in earth's atmosphere maintains a delicate balance that keeps the planet from getting too hot or too cold.

What does the greenhouse effect have to do with global warming? According to the IPCC's 2001 report, human activities are causing an increase in the levels of greenhouse gases in the atmosphere. An increase in greenhouse gases, particularly carbon dioxide, means more heat is being trapped by the atmosphere, leading to higher temperatures around the globe and the potential for global climate changes. Concentrations of atmospheric greenhouse gases have been steadily increasing since the beginning of the Industrial Revolution in the nineteenth century. The use of fossil fuels such as oil, gas, and coal has increased carbon dioxide levels by 30 percent. Fossil fuel use, waste dumps, increased agricultural production, and massive livestock operations have increased levels of methane by 240 percent. Modern industries such as aluminum production and the use of liquid coolants such as those in air conditioners have added new gases including perfluoromethane and chlorofluorocarbons (CFCs) to the greenhouse blanket. Because of the increased concentrations of greenhouse gases, states Maslin, "planet Earth is warming faster than at any other time in the past 1000 years and there is little doubt that human activity is to blame."

The Debate over Global Warming

Experts disagree about the causes of global warming, its severity, and how best to solve the problem. Kevin A. Shapiro, a neuroscience researcher based at Harvard, while acknowledging that earth's climate has warmed slightly in the last century, argues that this fact "more or less exhausts the scientific consensus. On every other important question—what the major causes of global warming are, what its effects will be, whether we should try to prevent it and, if so, how—there is considerable uncertainty." The use of computer simulations of weather patterns to predict the future extent and impact of global warming is particularly divisive. According to Shapiro, the use of these models has resulted in the accumulation of patchy and unreliable conclusions about human impact on earth's climate. Even the 2001 IPCC report, which was written by 122 lead authors and 515 contributing authors and was reviewed by another 450 scientists, does not represent total agreement among climate experts about the causes and effects of global warming. Meterologist Richard Lindzen, who was one of the 450 scientists who contributed to the report, notes that the "summary for policymakers" that is widely quoted in the media was written by only 14 of those 450 scientists—hardly a consensus. In an article about Lindzen and his views, *Newsweek* reporter Fred Guterl states that "many scientists agree that the IPCC, in its zeal to build the case for doing something about global warming, plays fast and loose with the science, glossing over uncertainty and pushing its conclusions too far."

Earth Is Getting Warmer

Although there is still some dispute about the effect human activities have on global warming and what is ultimately causing global climate change, the experts agree that, whatever the cause, earth is, indeed, getting warmer. Many climate scientists believe that allowing global warming to continue unchecked will have devastating consequences for Earth. Alexander E. MacDonald, a scientist with the National Oceanic and Atmospheric Administration, warns that warming temperatures could lead to devastating changes in weather patterns on a regional level. MacDonald predicts that

> summers may become much drier in the mid-continents of North America and Eurasia, with the potential to devastate some of the earth's most productive agricultural areas. The Arctic ice cap may disappear, a profound blow to a unique and fragile ecosystem. The Atlantic Ocean currents that warm Europe maybe disrupted. The West Antarctic Ice Sheet may collapse, leading to a rise in sea levels around the world.

Rising sea levels pose a threat to low-lying islands that could disappear completely under rising water. Warmer, drier summers in the world's most productive agricultural regions could devastate crop yields. Melting ice in the Arctic will endanger the habitat and food supply of animals such as polar bears. According to many experts on climate change famine, disease, and warfare could ultimately become widespread as water and other resources become scarce or disappear. As John T. Hardy, chair of the Department of Environmental Sciences at Western Washington University, states, there is no longer any doubt that "unprecedented changes in climate are taking place. If we continue on our present course, life on Earth will be inextricably altered. The very sustainability of the Earth's life-support system is now in question."

Not all scientists believe that the potential consequences of global warming will be so dire. Some predict that warmer temperatures will lead to increased crop yields, healthier forests, and an improved quality of life. In an interview for *U.S. News & World Report*, climatologist Craig Idso remarked that the extra carbon dioxide in the atmosphere "is going to be nothing but a boon for the biosphere. Plants will grow like gangbusters." Shapiro points out that early predictions about the consequences of global warming have not yet come to pass. In the 1980s, he relates, climatologists predicted that sea levels would rise twenty-five feet over the next century. "Under the worst-case scenario now envisioned by the IPCC," Shapiro states, "the oceans should rise no more than a foot over the next century, not nearly enough to pose a major threat."

The Danger of Stopping Global Warming

Some researchers believe that the consequences of attempting to slow global warming may be worse than the impact of the warming itself.

Attempts to control greenhouse gas emissions could end up hurting the world's economy. Indur M. Goklany of the Political Economy Research Center in Bozeman, Montana, writes that attempts to slow greenhouse gas emissions over the next several decades "could indirectly aggravate hunger and reduce public health services, either of which, separately or together, could increase mortality, particularly in developing countries." Goklany argues that there is no guarantee that controlling greenhouse gases "will provide net global benefits for public health or, separately, for the environment, but there is a good likelihood that it may well worsen both." For Goklany and other scientists who believe that global warming is not a serious problem, the best solution may be to do nothing.

Although most climate experts agree that global warming is occurring, no consensus has yet been reached on the scope and consequences of climate change. *Contemporary Issues Companion: Global Warming* provides various perspectives on this critical issue, including discussions of the research and science of global warming, the possible consequences of unchecked global warming, and potential solutions.

CHAPTER 1

UNDERSTANDING GLOBAL WARMING

RESEARCHERS INVESTIGATE THE GLOBAL WARMING PHENOMENON

Constanza Villalba

In the following selection, Constanza Villalba discusses the different techniques that climate researchers use to study how and why the earth's climate is changing. Villalba explains that climatologists can find evidence of variations in climate patterns over time by measuring differences in growth patterns of trees, accumulations of chemicals in coral, or layers of lake sediment. In addition to gathering information from the natural world, the author writes, researchers use sophisticated computer models that help predict how the climate may change in the future. These scientists are also studying the potential long-term consequences of a warming climate, she relates, including the ways in which plants, animals, and people may be affected. Villalba concludes by noting that while climate researchers are investigating both natural and man-made effects on the climate, most agree that human activity is at least partly responsible for global warming. Villalba is a writer for the Massachusetts Medical Society.

Like a modern-day druid—English accent and all—Ray Bradley asks trees to impart to him their knowledge of Earth's ancient mysteries. Since Bradley is a climatologist—as well as a professor and head of geosciences at UMass [the University of Massachusetts]—the mystery most intriguing him these days is the rapid heating up of Earth's atmosphere known as global warming.

With a group of eight colleagues in UMass's Climate System Research Center, which he founded in 1998, Bradley looks not only to trees, but to corals and lake sediments, to reconstruct the climatic history of the planet. Over the past several years his group has brought forward startling evidence that global warming is not only real and the evident result of human activity, but that its progress has been swift and substantial.

In two widely cited articles, one of them published in the journal *Nature* in 1998, Bradley and two other scientists charted a timeline of yearly average temperatures on Earth over the last 1,000 years. The timeline is graphic evidence of what he calls "a completely anomalous warming trend culminating in the 1990s." In fact, according to the team's calculations, 1998 was the hottest year of the millennium just past, and will likely be followed by even hotter years.

Bradley, whose silver hair and beard normally frame a placid expression, is visibly piqued by those who minimize the significance of global warming. His own sense of that significance drives his current efforts to demonstrate how Earth's climate has changed and why. Working from international data bases as well as his own research, Bradley and his confederates have compiled information derived from "proxies," or natural archives, in Canada, Russia, Bolivia, and numerous other locations around the globe. The proxy data represent a worldwide, collaborative effort by climatologists who have x-rayed, chemically analyzed, and visually scrutinized thousands of cylindrical cores taken from trees, corals, and frozen lake sediments.

Natural Climate Markers

The width and the density of tree rings, for example, vary with the interaction between species, geographic location, and the ephemeral conditions that make up climate: temperature, light, and the availability of water. In New England, for instance, a wide, dense ring on an Eastern Hemlock or a White Oak—both good proxy trees—suggests a warm, moist year. In the deserts of Arizona, where heat represents stress, a similar ring on a Foxtail Pine suggests a cooler year. And trees are affected by more than just climate, notes Bradley. They can, for example, be stifled by pest infestation or the lack of vital nutrients. So while each tree carries what Bradley calls a "climatic signal," it is "the job of the analyst to determine what part is due to climate and what part is due to other factors."

Climatic signals are also found in the rings of corals and the laminations of lake sediments. Yearly layers of coral, which grow atop the limestone exudate of their defunct predecessors, incorporate different amounts of strontium, calcium, and magnesium depending on the water temperature in which they grow. By measuring the ratios of these minerals, climatologists can extrapolate the temperatures that correspond to each year.

Ice cores, the annual accretions of which can remain clearly delineated for thousands of years, convey similar messages about temperature: for instance, in the relative amounts of two forms of oxygen isotope in each layer. "When water evaporates, more oxygen-16 than oxygen-18 is lost," explains one of Bradley's colleagues, Mark Abbott. "If you find a lot of oxygen-18 in a layer, the climate was colder at that time."

"Varved," or layered, lake sediments also convey climate history. In the Canadian high arctic, where Bradley and his team do fieldwork, there are lakes that remain frozen for most of the year. Each summer thaw, depending on the heat of the season, brings a rush or a trickle of melted snow. The speed and force with which that water moves determines the size of the particles it will wash into the lake, and which will settle into the lake floor. Therefore, layers of sediment with large, coarse chunks represent hot summers. Fine grains represent cool ones.

Deciphering Climatic Signals

In essence, climatologists must decipher a manuscript which has been written in a foreign language, and of which only the last chapter has been translated. The key to unlocking the climatic signals of any natural archive lies in that last chapter: in the fact that humans have been keeping explicit records of climate for the past hundred and fifty years. Using these records, climatologists can correlate the characteristics of modern trees, coral, and sediment with the known climates in which they were generated, and draw conclusions about how climate shaped them. Then, by a process called calibration, the findings can be applied to proxy data from years when no human record of climate exists.

The significance of Bradley's work, and the reason it received such widespread attention, is that the research which he published with colleagues Michael Mann, then at UMass, and Malcolm Hughes of the University of Arizona, was the first to apply such a comprehensive, proxy-based approach to the question of global warming.

What of those who say, in effect, "Oh, well—temperatures have always gone up and down"? Earth's current heat wave may be unprecedented by recent standards, but it has certainly been much hotter without the world coming to an end.

Rob DeConto, assistant professor of geosciences and an expert on the Cretaceous period, might seem to be lending aid and comfort to the lackadaisical when he observes that "when dinosaurs ruled the Earth, this was a mostly ice-free planet." Antarctica, DeConto observes, was completely forested a hundred million years ago.

"Yes, the Earth has been warmer than it is now," says DeConto. "But the point is that it was completely unrecognizable."

Using Computers to Predict Climate Change

DeConto's efforts to forecast how unrecognizable the Earth may become in the future involve the use of sophisticated computer climate models. Of particular interest to him is how living organisms affect climate. Until recently, he says, while climate models incorporated such environmental factors as the amount of heat emitted by the Sun and the chemical composition of the atmosphere, few accounted for biological impacts. When such models were tested against the past as revealed by proxy data, they proved inadequate.

For instance, according to the old, biology-free models, the interiors of Earth's continents should have been very cold during the Cretaceous. Yet paleontologists working far inland have found fossil remains of crocodilians—crocodile ancestors—who could never have survived such temperatures.

DeConto says that seeing Earth's surface and biology as interactive improves such models. For example, the forests that shrouded Earth's poles during the Cretaceous would not have reflected the Sun's rays as the polar ice caps do today: foliage traps heat in much the same way as a dark T-shirt on a hot summer day. Likewise, it may have been the vegetation of the ancient continental interiors that kept them hospitable to crocodile-types.

Among Earth's living constituents, human beings have been among the most interactive. According to Bradley and his colleagues, the planet's heating trend can be traced back to the industrial revolution, when human use of fossil fuels became commonplace. Burning coal, oil, or natural gas releases carbon dioxide and other compounds into the air; carbon dioxide is one of several atmospheric gases which literally blanket the Earth and prevent heat from dissipating. CO_2, along with methane and nitrous oxide, has become increasingly abundant in the atmosphere in the last two centuries, and Bradley, DeConto, Abbott, and virtually all scientists in this field agree that increasing levels of CO_2, combined with deforestation, are responsible for the recent monumental changes in temperature.

A transparency that Bradley uses in his talks on global warming makes graphic the differences between modern and pre-industrial amounts of atmospheric CO_2. Prior to 1850, he says, "carbon dioxide levels were at about 280 parts per million. Today they are about 360 parts per million." And if CO_2 in the atmosphere continues to increase at its current rate, it will double its pre-industrial level in the coming century.

The Consequences of Climate Change

One of the textbooks used by Karen Searcy, curator of the UMass herbarium, to teach Introductory Ecology supports DeConto's notion of an unrecognizable future world. If carbon dioxide levels were to double, it says, "beech trees presently distributed throughout all of the eastern United States and southeastern Canada would die back in all areas except northern Maine, northern New Brunswick, and Quebec." All of the plants and animals that populate Massachusetts, Searcy adds, could change to suit the climate. Species that need colder temperatures could migrate north, while others that have never grown [in Massachusetts] may flourish.

"One of the species that is predicted to migrate north is the sugar maple," says Searcy, "which would take the intensity out of our autumn foliage. You would see more russets and browns, less orange and red." And muted autumn colors, of course, would be among the more benign consequences of global warming. DeConto points to the melting of glaciers that could raise sea levels and devastate flat and low-lying coastal regions. (Boston's Back Bay, not to mention much of Bangladesh, would be at risk.) Fresh water from glaciers could also disrupt the churning flow of sea water that normally blunts extreme temperature changes. Perhaps most importantly, the planet is "getting closer and closer" to the limits of its food-producing capacity, DeConto says. "If the climate changes enough to impact an area that supports corn . . ." he shrugs, leaving his sentence uncompleted.

Such predictions for the future of the planetary environment are, of course, speculative. But in this case, they also come from a working understanding of climate, an understanding which continues to be deepened by studies at UMass's Climate System Research Center.

A Multidirectional Approach to Climate Research

Housed in an octagonal, multi-windowed room, . . . the center supports a multidirectional approach to climate. It is supported in turn by funding from the National Science Foundation, the National Oceanographic and Atmospheric Administration, and the Department of Energy.

Meteorological sensors with automatic data loggers, and tools for geologic coring and analysis, are among the resources gathered there for use by the university's climatologists.

These resources are used to study not only global warming, but how climate varies naturally. Abbott, especially, is interested in "differentiating between a normal climate with natural rhythms and what's man-made." Clearly, human use of fossil fuel is not the only factor driving changes in climate. Consider the 1991 eruption of Mount Pinatubo in the Philippines. Dust and ash particles from the eruption shrouded—literally shaded—the islands for months, producing an exceptionally cold summer.

More generally, says Abbott, the energy emitted by the Sun has been increasing since the early 19th century, and the variable distance and angle between the Sun and the wobbly Earth gradually changes over time. His research shows that water levels in Lake Titicaca, his study site on the border between Bolivia and Peru, have risen and fallen with the wobbling of the Earth on its axis. "The intertropical convergence zone—the low pressure belt that brings rain—follows the hottest spot on the continent," he says. When changes in the angle of Earth to Sun shift the warm zone to another part of the globe, the rains go with it. Notably, Abbott has found elevations of water levels in Venezuelan lakes that precisely coincide with the drops in Bolivia and Peru.

Regardless of the impact of natural factors on Earth's climate, the fact remains that humans are at least partially to blame for potentially devastating increases in temperature. What can we do? Sign the Kyoto protocol, says Bradley. Nations that sign this international agreement promise to reduce greenhouse gas emissions to 1990 levels by 2010. "It's not perfect," he says, "but it's a step in the right direction."

Bradley is well-acquainted with the argument that the protocol is a prohibitively costly approach to a threat that's at best remote. Not surprisingly, he disagrees. "We've made huge investments in the past to protect ourselves from fairly unlikely events like the Russian launch," he says. "Why not guard against an event that is slowly but undeniably creeping up on us?"

GLOBAL WARMING RESEARCH IN THE ARCTIC

Glenn Hodges

Why is the Arctic warming, and what does it mean for the earth's climate? In the following article, *National Geographic* writer Glenn Hodges describes his trip on a submarine in the Arctic with researchers who are trying to answer these questions. Scientists are concerned because the Arctic is currently experiencing a marked warming trend, Hodges relates, but the Arctic is such a complex environment that it is difficult for researchers to determine whether these changes are related to global warming. Nevertheless, he notes, climatologists and other researchers are gathering plenty of data to help them answer their questions about climate change: In addition to submarine voyages, researchers are utilizing sophisticated new technologies to gather climate data in the Arctic. Hodges explains that these experts hope to determine if Arctic warming will lead to catastrophic global climate change or if it is simply a natural part of an age-old cycle.

In a world that's been almost completely mapped, it's easy to forget why cartographers used to put monsters in the blank spots. Today we got a reminder. The submarine captain had warned us that we were in uncharted waters: "We're making the charts as we go along," he had said. "That's common in the Arctic." Yet the first days of our cruise through this ice-covered ocean, Earth's least explored frontier, were as smooth as you'd expect in this age of recreational adventure. Even when we passed over a mile-high mountain that no one on the planet knew existed, the reaction was one of quiet enthusiasm—"Neat."

That all changed when the sonar told us we were about to crash. The ship's loudspeaker bellowed "RED SOUNDING!"—a warning, the captain explained, that "you need to do something, or you're going to run aground." In that instant the U.S.S. Hawkbill's crew came face-to-face with the fact that they didn't know what their surroundings held for them. Outside the frenzied control room I asked the Chief of the Boat (COB) Gary Olivi if he'd ever encountered a red sounding. He

Glen Hodges, "The New Cold War," *National Geographic*, vol. 197, March 2000, p. 30.

hadn't. How long had he been a submariner? "Since 1983."

Fortunately the COB got a story for his grandkids and nothing more. After a few tense minutes it became clear that we had found not a mountain but a monster—one of those scary apparitions that dwell in unknown places. The main sonar had gone off-line, and a backup system picked up a false echo that registered as a seamount. We were safely above the bottom the whole time. This monster we dispatched for the cost of a few gray hairs—or in the case of the captain, Comdr. Robert Perry, "two years off my life." As Arctic monsters go, though, it wasn't a very big one.

Warming in the Arctic

The Arctic, you see, has warmed markedly in the past two decades, and scientists have only a hazy understanding of why this is happening and what it means—partly because climate questions are inherently hard to untangle and also because knowledge of the Arctic lags decades behind that of the world's other oceans. Covered by ice year-round, the Arctic is virtually inaccessible to ship traffic and has been the province largely of nuclear subs on cat-and-mouse missions for the past half century.

But the close of the Cold War opened a new door for Arctic research, and [in 2000,] for the fifth year in a row, a nuclear submarine is hosting a scientific mission in the Arctic as part of the SCICEX (Science Ice Expeditions) program, spearheaded by the United States Navy and the National Science Foundation. I'm on board the Hawkbill for the first leg of its six-week Arctic cruise. Stocked with scientists and special equipment, the 30-year-old attack sub will zigzag around the Arctic Ocean, mapping the seafloor while collecting data on temperature, currents, salinity, nutrients, and ice thickness.

Already SCICEX has more than doubled the world's store of Arctic Ocean data, and it comes just in time. The ocean's ice cover has thinned by an average of four feet—some 40 percent—since the 1960s, and satellite data show that the ice's reach has receded 5 percent. More recently, relatively warm Atlantic water has pushed 20 percent farther into the Arctic than scientists have ever seen—and that water is 1.6°F warmer than it was only a decade or so ago. Meanwhile, along the ocean's southern margin, the thin layer of frigid water that insulates the ice from that warmer Atlantic water has been thinning, and in some places it is absent altogether.

Given that the Poles are widely seen as bell-wethers of global climate change, this all looks very dramatic. But it may be just another imagined monster lurking in the blank spots of our knowledge. Perhaps the water regularly warms and cools and the ice regularly thins and thickens as atmospheric pressures and water currents oscillate. There's evidence to suggest that, but it's not conclusive. Although a 1997 accord gave scientists access to decades of historical Arctic data collected by the Soviet and U.S. governments, the record is far from complete and before 1950 largely nonexistent. So the questions remain: Will currents and temperatures revert to more familiar patterns? Or is the Arctic showing signs of global warming?

A Complex Problem

If the Arctic continues to warm, the consequences could be grave. Some scientists think there's a chance—remote but conceivable—that the ocean's summer ice cover could completely melt at some point in coming decades. "The absence of ice in the Arctic would completely change climate patterns for the Northern Hemisphere," says Dave Clark, a marine geologist at the University of Wisconsin. "In computer modeling if you take off the ice, even the circulation of the ocean reverses."

Some scientists think that the Arctic Ocean may have lost its summer ice 400,000 years ago, when the Earth was as warm as it is now. The Earth has a history of warming and cooling dramatically in just decades or even years as environmental factors amplify each other. In the Arctic, for instance, sea ice reflects most solar energy, but open water absorbs up to 90 percent. So as ice cover shrinks, the ocean absorbs more heat, potentially melting more ice until a cycle of increased heating and melting eliminates the permanent ice pack.

But this is a simple model, and the Arctic is no simple environment. "The problem in the Arctic is there's a lot of variability," says Mike Ledbetter, a program director at the National Science Foundation's Office of Polar Programs. "Conditions can be very different from one year to the next, so identifying trends is difficult." Drew Rothrock, a University of Washington research scientist who identified the thinning ice, says, "People may jump on this and say the ice cover is disappearing. Well, who knows? Everything may rebound now for the next ten years. I don't think you'd find many Arctic scientists willing to say, 'Yes, it's all melting up there, and in another decade we won't have any sea ice.' Only the future will tell us."

Looking for Clues from the Past

When the Hawkbill is not in the throes of an emergency, the best action can be found in the torpedo room, which for this mission has been transformed into a science center. Instrument monitors, racks of water samples, and assorted equipment line a narrow walkway running lengthwise through the garage-size room.

For this mission the Hawkbill is equipped with an array of instruments known as SCAMP—the Seafloor Characterization and Mapping Pod—which includes a side-scan sonar that produces high-resolution images of the ocean floor.

On the first morning of the cruise the chief scientist, Margo Edwards of the University of Hawaii, explains the first phase of our mission: to explore the Chukchi Plateau, a Denmark-size underwater feature about 700 miles north of the Bering Strait, and examine the seafloor for gouges made by ice sheets during past ice ages. "We're trying to get a handle on what the Arctic was like at the coldest point of the last ice age," she says.

So far no one has found strong evidence of ice sheet scours in this part of the Arctic Ocean. But not 24 hours into the trip I find her beaming in front of the main SCAMP monitor, looking at signs of ice sheet scours 1,200 feet below the surface. "I've never seen anything like this!" says Edwards, who has been studying marine geology for 14 years. The scours look like tracks from a thick-bristled broom dragged across a sandbox. One gouge is 60 feet deep. "Wow. I never thought the bathymetry would get this good this fast."

The next day it gets even better. Edwards finds what appears to be a moraine, a pile of debris deposited by an ice sheet. "It's pretty good evidence that an ice sheet came out this far." She asks the navigator to change course so that the sub can return to the area and map it more thoroughly. "The submarine is an ideal platform; there's no other way to do this."

Submarines can collect so much data so quickly that scientists will be busy analyzing the information from this and previous SCICEX cruises for years. But they're also working on new ways to collect Arctic data. Though the Navy plans to piggyback some scientific work on future Arctic missions, the last of the Sturgeon-class subs used for SCICEX cruises will be scrapped in 2001, and the Navy's shrinking sub fleet probably won't have room for science-only cruises in the near future.

After a week on the Hawkbill I disembark at the camp where I boarded—a half-dozen tents and plywood shacks on the sea ice 165 miles north of Barrow, Alaska. There two teams of scientists are working on projects to help fill the post-SCICEX void.

New Research Methods

"Ah, the smell of burning plastic," says Peter Mikhalevsky, the ice camp's chief scientist, as he walks into the tent where a three-man team from Scientific Solutions, Inc. (SSI), is trying to fix the latest malfunction in their project—a buoy for an autonomous underwater vehicle (AUV) designed to record ocean climate data. I've been watching these guys for a couple of days, thoroughly captivated by the long procession of breakdowns and foul-ups they've encountered.

"You're getting firsthand knowledge of what really goes on behind all those fancy equations and papers," says Armen Bahlavouni, the buoy's engineer.

With a projected range of more than 600 miles, far beyond that of any current AUV, the vehicle they're developing the buoy for will help monitor changes in the Arctic Ocean's temperature and salinity. But one of the big engineering obstacles is how to get the data out of an ice-covered ocean, and that's where SSI comes in. It's building a yard-long buoy that will carry data from the AUV to the ocean's surface. When the buoy hits the ice, a chemical reaction heats seawater in its nose cone until the steam melts through the ice. Then a transmitter emerges to send the data to a satellite.

From what they tell me, they're fighting an uphill battle to make this buoy work. They're confident they can do it, but not everyone else is. Peter Stein, president of SSI, says they met with a colleague at Woods Hole Oceanographic Institution who joked before their meeting that he'd give the buoy a snowball's chance in hell of working; after their meeting he upgraded his appraisal to "a snowball's chance in Phoenix."

After a series of leaky seals, broken switches, and burned-out pumps, we finally head to the test site—a hole in the ice a few hundred feet from camp. The pump runs, but nothing happens. Back in the tent Bahlavouni concludes that a pinched tube prevented acid from reaching a chemical. An easy thing to fix, he says, but "in the meantime we accidentally squirted acid on a conductor and probably shorted out the battery."

It may be just as well that the camp shuts down for an hour that afternoon. The hum of the generator stops, and everyone heads indoors to avoid crunching across the ice because the other science team—Peter Mikhalevsky and Mike Lents from Science Applications International Corporation—needs perfect quiet while receiving an acoustic transmission from a Russian source on the opposite side of the ocean, 1,600 miles away. In the science hut they'll lower a receiver array through a hole in the six-foot-thick ice to hear the signal. By timing how long it takes the signal to cross the ocean, they can determine the average temperature of the water it travels through. When the ACOUS (Arctic Climate Observations Using Underwater Sound) system is completed, with as many as three sources and six receivers (two of each will be in place by 2002), it will provide a broad view of temperature changes across the Arctic Ocean in real time, year-round—something even submarines can't do.

In a 1994 pilot project ACOUS's transmission signal traveled through the Atlantic water layer two seconds faster than predicted, based on historical climate records, indicating a temperature increase of 0.7°F. The first reading at this ice camp four days ago revealed another 0.9° increase since 1994, which is consistent with SCICEX submarine data. Today, when the signal comes, it verifies the latest reading. The system is working, and everyone is happy.

Science Never Sleeps

Meanwhile, back in the SSI tent a switch is broken, and the team has no idea what happened to it. "It figures," Bahlavouni says. "We hadn't changed that switch." They change it and head back for a second try.

Again the pump runs, but to no avail. Back in the tent Bahlavouni sees the problem; they've been using fresh water to test the flow through the tubes, but it's freezing in the 29° seawater. They pump the water out, position the buoy under the ice, and start it up. The pump runs, and a milky green cloud wafts through the water. The chemical is reacting.

"Yay! Hooray!" After a few short minutes steam squirts from a hole in the ice, and the buoy's nose cone pops up.

"We did it!" Stein shouts.

"I can sleep tonight," Bahlavouni says.

Fortunately science never sleeps. With so many eyes on the Arctic now, scientists will find ways to get the data they need to make sense of changes in the climate. Of course, everyone hopes that the Arctic Ocean will cool again, leaving us not with catastrophic climate change but simply with a better understanding of one of the planet's least known places.

SCIENTIFIC EVIDENCE FOR GLOBAL WARMING

Robert T. Watson

Robert T. Watson is the chief scientist and senior spokesperson on global warming for the World Bank, as well as the former chair of the Intergovernmental Panel on Climate Change. There is strong scientific evidence that human activities are contributing to global climate change, Watson argues in the following selection. While the author acknowledges that some scientific uncertainties still exist, he maintains that researchers have verified significant increases in the earth's temperature during the twentieth century. In addition, he asserts, complex global climate models show that human activities are indeed having a profound impact on the warming trend. According to Watson, unless human production of greenhouse gases is sharply curtailed, global warming will result in dramatic changes to the world's environment.

Do scientists now have compelling evidence of global warming? The simple answer is: "Yes." We have strong evidence that the climate is changing and that human activities were the primary cause of the changes during the 20th century.

First, we have detected change. Global-average temperature is rising, precipitation patterns are changing, glaciers are retreating, sea levels are rising and Arctic sea ice is thinning. Second, we can attribute most of the observed warming of the last 50 years to human activities rather than to changes in solar radiation or other natural factors. Third, because human activities will continue to change the atmosphere's composition throughout the 21st century, global warming can be expected to continue. This will result in significant projected increases in global-average temperature, in the number of hot days, in heavy precipitation events and in higher sea level.

In 1997, representatives from more than 100 governments met in Kyoto, Japan, and agreed that industrialized countries should decrease their emissions of greenhouse gases. This decision was based in large part on the conclusions in the 1995 Assessment Report of the Intergovernmental Panel on Climate Change (IPCC). This report presented a careful and objective analysis of all relevant scientific, technical and economic information. It was prepared and peer-reviewed by more than 2,000 experts in the appropriate fields of science from academia, government, industry and environmental organizations worldwide.

Human Activity Is Causing Climate Change

In 1995, as [in 2001], the overwhelming majority of governments and scientific experts recognized that while scientific uncertainties existed, strong scientific evidence demonstrated that human activities were changing Earth's climate and that further human-induced climate change was inevitable. Hence, scientists and governments alike recognized in 1995 and reaffirm today that the question is not whether climate will change in response to human activities, but rather where (regional patterns), when (the rate of change) and by how much (magnitude).

The scientific evidence also indicates that climate change will, in many parts of the world, adversely affect human health, ecological systems (particularly forests and coral reefs), and important socioeconomic sectors, including agriculture, forestry, fisheries, water resources and human settlements. Developing countries are the most vulnerable, primarily because a larger share of their economies are in climate-sensitive sectors, and they do not have the institutional and financial infrastructures to adapt to climate change.

Since 1995, confidence in the ability of models to project future climate change has increased. This is because of their demonstrated performance in simulating key features of the climate system across a range of space and time intervals, most particularly, their success in simulating the observed warming during the 20th century. Certainly, models cannot simulate all aspects of climate. For example, they still cannot account fully for the differences in the observed trends in surface and midtropospheric temperatures during the last two decades.

On Jan. 22 [2001], in Shanghai, China, the IPCC released its latest report on climate-change science. This report was prepared by more than 600 scientists, peer-reviewed by more than 300 expert reviewers and further peer-reviewed and approved by nearly 100 governments. [In April and May 2001], the IPCC will release its third assessment report on impacts and vulnerability and on options for reducing greenhouse gas emissions. Both the 1995 and 2001 IPCC reports say that the Earth's climate is warming, that human activities are implicated in the observed warming and that the Earth will warm several degrees Fahrenheit during the next 100 years as compared with only about 1 degree during the last 100 years.

However, [the 2001] report makes an even stronger case that human-induced climate change is a serious environmental issue. Specifically, the report concluded, "Globally the Earth's climate is warmer today than at any time during the last 140 years. Direct ocean- and land-surface temperature measurements indicate that the global-average surface temperature has increased by 1.1 percent, or 0.4 F, since about 1860, with nighttime minimum temperatures warming at twice the rate of daytime maximum temperatures, with the land areas warming at twice the rate of the oceans, and with the 1990s being the warmest decade."

Temperatures Are Rising

The temperature increase in the Northern Hemisphere in the 20th century was greater than for any other century in the last 1,000 years. A new analysis from direct and indirect data (including tree-ring and coral-reef records) shows the temperature increase in the 20th century is greater than that for any other century during the last 1000 years and that temperatures now are warmer than at any time during this period. This further demonstrates that the climate of the 20th century was unique. There is new and stronger evidence that most of the observed warming during the last 50 years is attributable to human activities, primarily the use of fossil fuels and deforestation. This state-ment, which is based on recent theoretical modeling and new data-analysis techniques, is much stronger than the pioneering finding made in the 1995 report that "the balance of evidence suggests a dis-cernible human influence on global climate."

A comparison of observed changes in temperature with simulations from several complex global-climate models shows that 20th-century climate changes cannot be explained by internal variability and nat-ural phenomena. Simulations of climatic effects of changes in solar radiation and volcanic eruptions indicate that these natural phenom-ena may have contributed to the observed warming in the first half of the 20th century. But they cannot explain the warming in the latter half of the 20th century. In contrast, simulations that account for the impacts of both natural phenomena and human activities can account for both the time sequence and large-scale geographic patterns in sur-face temperature, as well as the trend in global-mean temperature.

Many observed changes in the Earth's climate are consistent with global-scale warming attributable to human influences. These include changes in precipitation, increases in sea level and oceanic tempera-tures, shrinking mountain glaciers, decreasing snow and ice cover and thinning Arctic sea ice.

Greenhouse Gas Emissions Are Increasing

The atmospheric concentrations of carbon dioxide and most other greenhouse gases are projected to increase significantly during the next 100 years. Emissions of greenhouse gases and sulfur dioxide will depend on a number of factors, including changes in population, eco-nomic growth and technological changes. But total cumulative carbon-dioxide emissions from all sources between 1990 and 2100 are projected to increase—in the absence of international action to address climate change—to a level of 770 to 2,540 billion tons of carbon. In contrast, total cumulative emissions between 1800 and the present have been about 400 billion tons of carbon. Despite the uncertainty in future emissions, all plausible projections suggest a significant increase in the atmospheric concentration of carbon dioxide, rising to a level of 540 to 970 parts per million (ppm) by 2100. Compare this with the preindustrial concentration of 280 ppm and the current concentration of about 368 ppm.

The atmospheric concentrations of sulfur dioxide are, in most cases, projected to decrease during the next 100 years. Sulfur-dioxide emissions, which tend to cool the atmosphere, are projected to range from about 11 million to 93 million tons per year, in contrast with 1990 emissions ceiling of about 70 million tons. In general, these projections are much lower than those in 1992 because most countries likely will try to reduce sulfate acid deposition. These lower projections enhance the magnitude of climate change by reducing the sulfate-aerosol cooling effect.

Globally, average surface-air temperatures are projected to rise 2.5 F to 10.4 F between 1990 and 2100, with most land areas warming more than the global average by up to 40 percent. A simple climate model simulating the response of seven complex global-climate models projects globally averaged surface-temperature increases of 2.5 F to 10.4 F between 1990 and 2100 for the full range of plausible trends in greenhouse gas and sulfur-dioxide emissions. This range of projected temperature change between 1990 and 2100 is higher, by 1.8 F to 6.3 F, than that reported in the assessment report, primarily because of the lowering of projected sulfur-dioxide emissions.

The Global Impact of Climate Change

Globally averaged precipitation is projected to increase, but both increases and decreases will occur depending on the specific global region. Warmer temperatures will enhance evaporation and precipitation by a few percent under all plausible emissions scenarios. Precipitation is projected to increase in both summer and winter over high-latitude regions; in winter over northern mid-latitudes, tropical Africa and Antarctica; and in summer over South and East Asia. Conversely, precipitation is projected to decrease in winter over Australia, Central America and Southern Africa. However, a key finding is that more-intense precipitation events are very likely over most regions of the world, consistent with changes already measured during the 20th century in northern mid and high latitudes. In addition, an increased risk of droughts and floods associated with the El Niño phenomena is very likely, even if there is no change in the intensity of the El Niño phenomena.

Global sea level is projected to rise by about 4 inches to 35 inches between 1990 and 2100. The top end of this range is quite close to the range projected in the 1995 IPCC assessment despite the higher temperature projections, primarily because of lower estimated contributions from Greenland and Antarctica.

In conclusion, the recent IPCC report provides strong evidence for human influence on the Earth's climate system. The good news is that the majority of experts believe significant reductions in net greenhouse-gas emissions are technically feasible. This is because of an extensive array of cost-effective technologies and policy measures in the energy supply, energy demand, agricultural and forestry sectors. In particular, the cost of reducing carbon-dioxide emissions for developing countries significantly can be lowered by industrialized countries purchasing "carbon credits" from developing countries which use the monies for abatement of carbon-dioxide emission. The bad news is that not only the climate is changing because of human activities, but evidence is mounting that ecosystems are as well. Given the fact of compelling scientific evidence, it is time for nations to determine how best to respond.

SCIENTIFIC SKEPTICISM ABOUT GLOBAL WARMING

Elizabeth Royte

In the following selection, Elizabeth Royte discusses the work of atmospheric science professor John Christy. As Royte relates, Christy is considered a maverick in the climate field because he is one of the few researchers who not only argues that humans have not caused global warming but also doubts that the earth is warming at all. Royte explains how Christy and a fellow scientist developed a new technique to measure temperature variations in the earth's atmosphere rather than relying on temperature readings taken on the ground. The data that Christy collected indicated that the earth's atmospheric temperature was cooler than expected—a finding that contradicted much previous research. While Christy did find a slight warming trend, the author notes, he believes it is due to natural causes and will not result in important climate changes. Royte is a freelance writer whose work has appeared in several publications, including *Discover, Outside, National Geographic*, and *Life*.

On an autumnal Sunday morning in suburban Huntsville, Alabama, the sun streams through the second-floor windows of a Baptist church classroom. Eight men and women sit in folding chairs, eyes focused on John Christy, the leader of their Bible-study group. Dressed in khaki pants and a short-sleeved shirt, Christy flips through the pages of Genesis. He's talking about Adam and Eve, about the difference between God and his creation. "All God created is precious," he says. "And humans are the most precious part of creation."

The others nod. They know Christy as a dedicated member of the church and a mellow-toned bass in its choir. Some of them know he's a scientist, and some may even know that he puts more faith in evolution as an explanatory theory than in creationism. But only those closest to Christy know the extent to which his science and his religion are intertwined—and how much his double life has helped shape the most heated scientific debate of the past 20 years.

A Scientific Maverick

A professor of atmospheric science at the University of Alabama in Huntsville, Christy is a member of the Intergovernmental Panel on Climate Change (IPCC) established by the United Nations [in 1988]. As such, he is one of the world's preeminent experts on atmospheric conditions, one whose research informs our basic understanding of climate change. Yet Christy is also something of a maverick. Years ago he cast doubt on the idea that global warming is caused by humans—or that the phenomenon exists at all—and he has only grown more skeptical as most other atmospheric scientists have grown more certain.

[In the fall of 2000], as the IPCC was preparing to announce, in stronger terms than ever before, that Earth is warming at an unprecedented rate and that people are the cause, Christy was declaring exactly the opposite. "The usual predictions show escalating atmospheric temperatures, and we're just not seeing that rise," he says. "This indicates that the cause of recent surface warming may be due to factors other than human activities."

Contrarians are never in short supply where global warming is concerned. But Christy is unique for both the quality of his science and the depth of his moral fervor. First, he backs up his hypotheses with rigorously vetted data from satellites and weather stations around the globe. Second, his opposition to emissions controls is rooted in compassion: As a Baptist missionary in Africa 27 years ago, Christy witnessed how the energy policies of large nations can devastate small communities dependent on fossil fuels.

Today, inspired for a moment by the lesson from Genesis, he can't resist an aside to his students. "Now, some extreme environmentalists, they say that a whale is more important than your child. These people," he says, leaning forward over a low table, blue eyes twinkling, "they want us to live in the Stone Age." He shakes off the crazy thought and returns to Adam and Eve.

From his earliest years, Christy trained his eyes on the sky: "I was a weather weenie," he says. He remembers watching storms gather above the Sierras from his family's house in Fresno, California. When rain fell, he climbed onto the roof to take measurements. In the 1960s, he recorded 75 different weather variables, including four daily readings of wind speed and direction, cloud type, and barometric pressure, all using a homemade weather station. He analyzed the observations statistically and wrote a computer program in Fortran that could make three-day forecasts based on the data.

Devastating Energy Policies

Christy was also active in the Baptist church from an early age. His parents were devout, and he attended religious retreats and taught Bible school to the children of tourists in the Sierras. Through high school and college, Christy leaned toward the ministry, but a professor advised him to study what he loved. In 1973, at the age of 22, with a fresh B.A. in math and a low draft number, Christy opted out of the Vietnam War by joining a Baptist mission in the Kenyan village of Nyeri, in the highlands outside Nairobi.

Christy went to Kenya to teach high-school science, but he soon found that he was powerless to offer villagers the economic help they really needed. The Arab oil embargo had sent energy prices soaring. "I saw the number of nighttime accidents go up because a rumor spread that turning off your headlights conserved gas," Christy remembers. He also watched as sick villagers got sicker because they couldn't afford to take taxis to the hospital. He knew of one school that closed because its Texas patrons, strapped for cash, couldn't send their monthly checks.

That experience forever shaped his views on energy policy. "Disrupting the lives of those whose existence is too often literally hanging by a thread causes the kind of suffering that the average policy maker or activist never sees," he told the House Small Business Committee in 1998. "I have seen it. It is real, and it is devastating." Christy's wife, Alice Babbette Joslin, saw it too. She met him while in Kenya, where she was also a teacher and missionary, and after two years they returned to the United States and were married. Christy went on to earn his master of divinity at Golden Gate Baptist Theological Seminary in Mill Valley, California. Then he moved to South Dakota, started a church, and endured four frigid winters, one of them the coldest in a decade and the second coldest in a century.

Studying the Weather

All the while, the gods of weather were calling too. Like the Johnny Appleseed of weather weenies, Christy scattered rain gauges wherever he went, and in 1982 he finally resumed his childhood passion. He earned his master's and Ph.D. degrees in atmospheric sciences from the University of Illinois. He taught at Illinois's Parkland College, then settled at the University of Alabama in Huntsville, where he is director of the Earth System Science Center. Outside his neat brick house, a rain gauge rises at the edge of a sloping driveway. The neighbors thought it an odd place to set up a basketball net.

The Christys have two children—Alison, who recently graduated from Auburn University with a degree in applied mathematics, and Brian, who is majoring in physics at Auburn and has already presented two posters at a conference. Christy swears he didn't predetermine his offspring's career paths, but he does joke that he wouldn't talk to them until they could factor polynomials.

"There's a lot of statistics talk around here," his wife says one afternoon, after a lunch of stewed chicken, cheddared broccoli, corn, and green Jell-O. "Last Christmas, we had a present that wasn't labeled. I picked it up and said, 'What are the odds that this is for me?' Well, everyone chimed in with a very precise answer."

To most people, numbers are hard and immutable, but Christy knows that they're subject to interpretation—and too often misinterpretation. For years, he listened as politicians and scientists spoke of rising global temperatures. But he questioned the data behind their predictions. He knew that buildings had been erected around thermometers and that nearby forests had been cut down, driving up recorded temperatures independently of any global climate change. He knew that scientists didn't have a way to get accurate readings of temperatures above the Earth's surface, so they didn't know what was happening to the lower troposphere—the first five miles of air hovering above Earth.

To fill in that vast gap, Christy began to work with Roy Spencer, a satellite meteorologist at NASA's Marshall Space Flight Center in Huntsville, extracting data from polar-orbiting satellites. The satellites carried instruments that measure the intensity of microwave radiation emitted by oxygen. Weather forecasters had used this data in a limited way to record temperatures at 20 different levels of the atmosphere but never to get a global average for the troposphere. Figuring out how to infer tropospheric temperature from the data was Christy and Spencer's genius.

Proving Climate Models Wrong

In theory, if the atmosphere heats up like a giant greenhouse, then the troposphere ought to be warming as rapidly as the Earth's surface, if not faster. According to Spencer and Christy's satellite data, however, the lower troposphere was surprisingly cool. Since 1979, it had warmed only 0.2 degrees Fahrenheit, whereas the surface had warmed between 0.48 and 0.7 degrees Fahrenheit. The disparity suggested to Christy that prevailing climate models were wrong.

As soon as he published his figures in 1990, Christy was attacked in scientific journals, in the media, and as the years passed, on the Web. There were questions about satellite drift, orbital decay, instrument temperature, and other possible biases. While environmentalists accused him of destroying the planet, industry public relations officers gleefully distributed Christy's statistics on the Internet. Of the two contingents, Christy says, "I'm more upset with environmental advocacy groups who lie about my data, who say it's inaccurate." He says one employee of NASA's Mission to Planet Earth program, which studies climate change, told him, "I'm paying people to come at you with bricks and bats."

"The critics kept popping up, like dragons," Christy says. One by one, he and Spencer slew them. Their weapon: math. For months on end, the men identified and quantified possible sources of error, applied nonlinear-trend reconstruction algorithms, and corrected least-squares regressions. They calibrated one satellite against another and, finally, validated their corrected numbers with readings from radiosondes—weather balloons that have been collecting data worldwide since 1958. In the end, he says, the errors fell to less than a tenth of a degree for the 20-year period.

Eventually, scientific opinion turned in Spencer and Christy's favor. In 1996, the American Meteorological Society presented them with an award for "fundamentally advancing our ability to monitor climate." In 1997, the Hadley Centre for Climate Prediction and Research in England independently verified their data. "We have nine data sets and they're absolutely confirmed," Christy says. "They're dead-on."

Conflicting Conclusions

Sitting in his office today, surrounded by weather charts and climate bulletins, Christy looks as preternaturally neat as his data: lean and square-chinned, his hair and push-broom mustache trimmed with diamond-edged precision. He's not especially tall, but he gives the impression, when he's excited by his topic, of having rocked onto his toes. At 49, he seems at least a decade younger.

On the walls, Christy has hung computer-generated charts of his times on 5-kilometer, 10-kilometer, and marathon runs. (When he's not working or running, Christy heads for the North Carolina hills, to pan for gold with a sluice box and shovel.) On the door is an Al Gore–signed letter from the Democratic National Committee, asking, "Won't you join us?"

The letter is posted as a dig at Gore's belief in global warming. But it points to a bitter irony at the core of Christy's research: While his data have won praise, his conclusions have not. In a report released on January 12 [2000], the National Research Council declared that the disparity between surface and troposphere temperatures is probably real, but that it's difficult to say why it exists or what it means.

More galling for Christy is the report released [in 2001] by the IPCC—a definitive 1,000-page document that Christy himself coauthored—that essentially contradicts his interpretation of the surface data. The burning of fossil fuels has "contributed substantially to the observed warming over the last 50 years," the report concludes. Moreover, it warns that temperatures could rise even higher than previously predicted—possibly 11 degrees over the next century.

Christy and IPCC members like James E. Hansen, director of NASA's Goddard Institute for Space Studies, agree that temperatures on the surface and in the troposphere don't necessarily move in lockstep and that they may need 50 years to converge. But Hansen believes—based on projections from current radiosonde readings—that the troposphere will continue to warm. The discrepancy that Christy found, he says, will disappear as climate models and measurements improve.

Christy thinks it equally likely that the Earth's surface will cool.

The surface warming that alarms so many atmospheric scientists is, to Christy, well within the realm of natural variation, or measurement error. "Most of this warming occurred in the early part of the 20th century, before humans had boosted concentrations of greenhouse gases," he says. Sunspots, volcanic eruptions, El Niños, variations in aerosols, water vapor, carbon dioxide and methane from living creatures, and other unknown factors may all tweak the planet's temperature up and down, Christy says. His satellite data show that the average temperature of the United States has been slightly higher recently than in previous years, but the average temperature of the southern hemisphere has been lower. When hot and cold spells are seen from a global perspective, he concludes, they eventually even out.

Precautionary Measures

Such positions have kept Christy in the distinct minority of scientists. Most climate researchers see retreating glaciers, thinning polar-sea ice, and warmer nights as evidence of human influence. The [2001] IPCC report acknowledges the uncertainty over tropospheric temperatures, but its more dire predictions are based on new temperature data gathered in the last few years, on improvements in computer models, and on a better understanding of how particulates affect climate. "In legitimate climate circles," says Brandon MacGillis of the National Environmental Trust, "there is no debate on the way humans have warmed the planet. It's happening."

Whatever their views on global warming, many scientists believe that precautionary measures are a win-win undertaking: If they don't prevent rising temperatures, they will at least take advantage of some hard-won social and political momentum to clean up the environment. Christy has no complaint with reducing toxic emissions like methane, sulfur dioxide, and nitrous oxide. "I care about our environmental problems," he says, "if they're scientifically based and put into perspective with global environmental problems. But what I see is people in the Northeast and the West trying to control how others live." He says the environmental effects of curbing greenhouse-gas emissions "are likely to be minuscule," while the social effects could be disastrous.

Christy is especially concerned about one oft-mentioned scheme for reducing greenhouse emissions: a carbon tax that would raise the price of fossil fuels until consumption goes down. He believes the tax would wreak havoc on poor areas by indirectly raising the prices of goods and services. "In Africa I saw a society living on the edge," he says. "You tweak one thing and it rapidly begins to disintegrate. A villager might not buy fuel, but the bicycle he wants could end up costing far too much for him to buy." He contends that the best thing for third-world countries that burn wood for fuel and heat is to build coal-fired power plants. "Cheap and accessible energy means better and longer lives. It means scientific and societal advances; it enhances health and security."

Many environmentalists would counter that the best schemes for reducing global warming would actually benefit the third world. The 1997 Kyoto Protocol, for instance, would allow countries with few CO_2 emissions to sell "emissions credits" to polluter nations like the United States. Tellingly, 30 countries have ratified the protocol, all nonindustrialized. Yet Christy, despite all his concern for the third world, still sides with the industrial nations. The United States "must remain robust," he insists, "with continued access to cheap energy." The Kyoto Protocol requires that by 2008 industrialized countries reduce their emissions to 5 percent below 1990 emissions levels, but Christy says that would cause "severe economic depressions."

Avoiding Bias

To keep politics from appearing to bias his science, Christy refuses support from industry groups. He works strictly with funding from NASA, the National Oceanic and Atmospheric Administration, the Department of Energy, the Department of Transportation, and the state of Alabama. But he is driven by a fundamental, religious belief that human life is "precious above all else," and his doubts about global warming can almost seem like an outgrowth of his distaste for any centralized government action. Asked what he would do if his data did show the troposphere warming in lockstep with the Earth's surface, he seemed genuinely at a loss. "I guess I'd still be skeptical about forecasts of catastrophe," he said. "That's my nature."

In the meantime, his skepticism has earned him more attention than anything he has ever done. Beginning in the mid-1990s, he visited Washington, D.C., at the behest of congressional committees, to present scientific testimony. He appeared on television and gave radio and newspaper interviews. "It was fun," he says. "I was the first person in my family to go to college, and I never imagined that because I know about climate and Fortran I'd be giving advice to the U.S. government."

Does a thirst for publicity—for being the star underdog—help drive Christy's predictions? "I recognize that feedback process, and I try to avoid it," he says. "I'm not going to ignore data. Most people at the bureaucratic level synthesize the work of others. But I write code, I look at numbers, I read and review papers. I would hope I'm objective, but I'm human." He pauses, then adds, "And the opportunity to do this is a thrill."

Gathering More Data

On a warm Monday morning, Christy takes a rare field trip, driving west from Huntsville to weather station Decatur 5SE. He wants to look at the setup, to see what factors might be influencing readings.

It's rural here, just 20 minutes outside Huntsville, and cotton fields stretch to the horizon.

Standing next to a collection of instruments—two thermometers, one anemometer, and rain and humidity gauges—Christy does a 360-degree turn. "We're surrounded by fields, but there's no natural forest cover here," he says, "so we'll get warmer daytime temperatures in the summer and cooler temperatures in the winter."

On a shelf back in Christy's office sits a box of state weather records dating from 1893. While many researchers consult the temperatures noted on the dog-eared pages, few have bothered to read the handwritten notes in the record. Christy's main concern is the records' consistency through time. The notes tell him that a station has moved 20 feet east, that a new observer was trained, that no one came to work on the weekend, that blacktop now surrounds the gauges. Such information creates anomalies that break up a homogeneous set of numbers.

If surface temperatures appear to be warming, Christy says, consider the context. "Creeping urbanization has a significant effect on the appearance of a warming Earth," he says. Cities are always warmer than the global average, particularly at night. Surface measurements are also unevenly distributed. There are more gauges in the northern hemisphere than the southern; we don't have reliable climate data for remote desert, ocean, and rain-forest areas. "This variance is the bane of our field," he says.

Christy climbs back into a university van and heads for another weather station 10 minutes away. Belle Mina 2N casts its shadow over hay fields. Three feet above the rain tower, outfitted with the latest in thermistors, sits a galvanized bucket, eight inches in diameter, topped with a funnel. "That's your basic rain gauge," Christy says. "Precipitation falls, and you stick a thin wooden ruler into the bucket to measure it. It always works." The contrast between low-tech and high is striking. In his office, Christy grooms and massages numbers downloaded from orbiting satellites; in the field, he's got volunteers poking measuring sticks into buckets. Of 10,000 such weather stations spread around the planet, a global data set is made.

Two weeks after his visit to Decatur 5SE and Belle Mina 2N, Christy goes to Asheville, North Carolina, for a workshop on improving balloon data. A day after his return, he's got big news. "We just had the earliest frost on record in Huntsville," he crows over the telephone. "It was 29 degrees on Monday night." He doesn't say so, but one gets the feeling he's glad.

GLOBAL WARMING RESULTS FROM NATURAL CAUSES

Sallie Baliunas, interviewed by James Glassman

James Glassman is the host of Tech Central Station, a public policy Web site. In this selection, he interviews astrophysicist Sallie Baliunas of the Harvard-Smithsonian Center for Astrophysics about the causes of global warming. Baliunas asserts that recent increases in the earth's temperature are linked to natural changes in the energy output of the sun. Because the temperature of the earth has fluctuated throughout its history, she explains, it should not be assumed that current warming trends are caused by human activities. According to Baliunas, scientific models of climate change have failed to take into account all the potential variables—including the influence of the sun—which has led to an inaccurate emphasis on the role of industrial pollutants. Nevertheless, she maintains, dire predictions about the consequences of global warming continue to be publicized, in spite of a lack of scientific consensus regarding the seriousness of the phenomenon.

Debate on the causes of predicted global warming usually revolves around climate models constructed by researchers. But can those models account for all the variables the universe has to offer? Not really, according to Dr. Sallie Baliunas of the Harvard-Smithsonian Center for Astrophysics, who points out that the sun is a variable not to forget.

"The science altogether is unsettled, but we know for sure that the models that make the predictions into the future are exaggerating the warmth," Dr. Sallie Baliunas tells Tech Central Station Host James Glassman.

Baliunas points out that increases in magnetism at the center of our solar system correlate quite strongly with temperature rises here on Earth. She also notes the difficulty of this scientific enterprise, saying: "There are something like 5 million parameters that have to go into a good climate model, and it has to compute for a time longer than the age of the universe if we wanted to know something."

Sallie Baliunas, interviewed by James Glassman, "Harvard Expert Debunks Global Warming Models," *Consumers' Research Magazine*, vol. 84, May 2001, p. 20. Copyright © 2001 by Consumers' Research, Inc. Reproduced by permission.

She and Glassman talked in Boston about the science, the uncertainty, and the sun's perhaps overlooked influence on climate change.

Prior Incidence of Global Warming

James K. Glassman: Dr. Baliunas, we've heard that temperatures have increased on Earth over the last century. Now, is our assumption essentially that they had been stable before that?

Sallie Baliunas: The temperature of the Earth has increased over the last 100 years. We have instruments—thermometers—at the surface of the Earth that tell us that. The warming began early in the 20th century, late in the 19th century. But before that, there was a very long, protracted cooling that began in the 14th century that continued to the mid-19th century—a 500-year relative cold spell called the Little Ice Age. Before that, 800 or 1,000 years ago—the early part of the second millennium—the temperature was even higher than today, worldwide.

So you're saying there was global warming before the 20th and 21st centuries?

Yes.

Well, they didn't have SUVs then?

No.

Why was the Earth heating up?

One property of climate is change. The temperature of the Earth has changed dramatically in some cases. And it's changed relatively greatly in the last 1,000 years even.

How can you tell?

The thermometers go back only about 100 years or so over some substantial portion of the Earth. Then we have to rely on other records, things that help us reconstruct the climate. For example, growth of tree rings is usually retarded during cold times or more advanced during warm times. So by boring into trees scientists can tell where there have been milder periods or cooler periods. And then there are many other indicators. Glaciers advance and retreat—mountain glaciers, polar glaciers. Coral growth rings tell us about the temperature of the ocean. There are many such indicators that go back thousands of years.

The Effect of the Sun

So if there was global warming way back, way before the 20th century, and it wasn't the result of spewing gases into the air, that is to say man-made global warming, then what caused it?

That's the big question. We need to answer the question: What are all the causes of climate change, natural climate change, that is, non-manmade? Look back in time, before the time when most of the carbon dioxide had been put in the air, you still see natural changes of a degree or so over decades or centuries, which is on the order of what the 20th century's warming has been.

Now to answer your question: We've been looking at changes in the sun's energy output, and we can evaluate changes in the sun's energy output going back as far as 10,000 years by looking at tree rings, interestingly enough. And when we do that, we see the ups and downs of the climate of the last 1,000 years and even of the 20th century match very well with the changes of temperature.

In other words, what you're saying is that because of activity on the surface of the sun, the Earth is warming up?

Right. When the sun's magnetism is strong, the sun's energy output is higher and the Earth is warmer. We see that as a fact. We measured that carefully over the last 20 years with satellites from the Earth, and we measured it indirectly going back 400 years, 1,000 years, and 10,000 years.

So in effect there are times when the sun is warmer than at other times?

Yes, and that warmth means the climate of the Earth warms.

A Strong Correlation

Now, have you actually correlated the activity of the sun with this magnetism that you're talking about, with the rise of temperatures on Earth?

Yes, the correlation is very strong. For the temperature records going back on Earth, we can reconstruct the northern hemisphere for about 250 years or so. And the ups and downs of temperature match almost exactly the ups and downs and change in magnetism, and so the energy output of the sun. As the sun warms and cools, the Earth's temperature is responding. And it doesn't take much of a change of the sun either—only about a few tenths of a percent of its energy output—to cause these temperature swings.

So, for example in the 1300s was there a period of global warming, climate change with temperatures rising? Was there solar activity then?

With records going back 1,000 years of solar magnetism, and the warm period certainly was in effect from about the years 1000 to 1200, maybe 1300 was about the edge of it, then there started a cooling. That 200- or 300-year period, the sun was much more active, magnetically, and we think, therefore, much brighter energetically than it is today. And then the magnetism declined into a long period of very low magnetism, lower energy output, and in step with these major changes in the Earth's climate over the last 1,000 years.

Has there been solar activity over the last 100 years that would correlate with the temperature on Earth?

Yes, it correlates almost exactly with the temperature on Earth. The sun is as magnetically active as it's been in our direct telescope records of the sun since the days of Galileo. So the magnetism of the sun has been rising gradually, and it was especially sharp early in the 20th century, coincident with this rise in temperature on the Earth.

Now there were declining temperatures from the 1940s through the mid-70s. Was there a lack of magnetism?

Yes, from about the 1930s, the 1940s, the sun's magnetism waned a little bit and has since picked up a little bit.

Estimating the Sun's Impact

What you're saying is that solar activity is causing global warming?

We are looking to find all the causes of natural change of the climate of the Earth, the sun being one of them. That way we can subtract out the natural changes and look for the human signal. We see, essentially, no signal of human activity.

Most of the changes that we see line up with the changes in the sun. Now there's some uncertainty, so there may be a human signal. But if there is, it's quite tiny.

What do your colleagues think of this idea?

It's very interesting. many of the climate models now try to incorporate the effect of the sun on them. Our next stumbling block is what exactly is the mechanism for change on the sun, and how does the Earth respond to that.

We think first of changes in the total energy output of the sun, but that's not the only way the sun changes. Different wavelengths of light are changing, and there are also high energy particles coming out of the sun, changing in step with magnetic changes. Some scientists have thought that those particles, for example, produce changes in cloud cover on Earth and change the temperature. We have to understand that before we can make a good estimate of what the sun's impact is. Right now everyone is struggling with the causes.

Your colleagues, fellow astrophysicists, don't say, "Oh, this is some sort of silly idea"?

No, astronomers know the sun is a variable star.

But, already, a lot of journalists or a lot of people who politicize this issue don't understand that?

They don't understand it, yeah. But it'll take time for their education.

Let me ask you about ice at the North Pole. According to the global warming theory, it should be melting rapidly. But you say that ice isn't cooperating with that theory?

No, neither ice nor temperature is cooperating with the model predictions. You're so right that the models, the computer output, say that the North Pole should be warming dramatically and rapidly. It hasn't been. It's really been cooling. Ice packs have been growing. There's just been no evidence that the Poles have been warmer. And to go look at, say, cracks in the ice or the calving of an iceberg and then to work backwards from that and say that has a human cause, that's just bad logic.

As a scientist, how do you react to journalistic coverage of this issue?

I try to read it all because people want to know the answer. But there's a sociology to journalism that I don't subscribe to, and so I'm not a journalist. That sociology is that scary stuff sells newspapers.

And you're a scientist, so you want to find out what's really going on?
Scientists have to go by the facts.

A History of Warming

How much warming have we actually seen in the last 100 years?
There's been about a half a degree centigrade or a degree Fahrenheit warming. Most of that warming occurred early in the century, before the greenhouse gases by human activities were added to the atmosphere.

And is this the first time we've ever seen warming on this planet?
Oh no. (laughs) No. There have been times—the warming in the late 19th century, especially in the high polar regions—that can't be caused by the human-induced greenhouse gases. That was much stronger than any warming we've seen in recent decades. Now with ice core records—drilled in the high latitudes and polar regions to pull up 100,000, 200,000 years of ice core layers that tell the temperature—there's some warmings and coolings there over decades that are astonishing: several degrees. Not manmade.

And when you say every decade, you're talking about thousands of years ago or hundreds of years ago?
Some of these episodes during the Little Ice Age, for example, were just several hundred years ago.

Unsettled Science

If there is an increase in temperature, and as you say it has been a half a degree over the past century, people are worried that maybe that is the beginning of a big acceleration of temperature. Do you think the science is settled at this point about whether we'll have any more global warming?
I think the science is settled that the predictions are exaggerated. There is maybe some human-made warming, but it's going to be so small that it's going to be lost in the natural variability. And that's the conclusion from science.

The acid test of all this is the last 22 years of satellite measurements made of the lower layer of air of the Earth. That layer of air should be warming quite rapidly. It's where the carbon dioxide greenhouse effect should be taking place. That layer there has not seen a big warming trend. It's seen ups and downs but there's been no net trend. That layer of air has to warm first according to the models. Then it, in turn, warms the surface. Now we've seen a little bit of warming of the surface, but it can't be caused by that carbon dioxide effect in that atmospheric layer, which shows no warming. You can't bypass the lower layer of air and warm the surface by carbon dioxide effect. So the satellite measurements, which are precise and validated by independent balloon measurements everyday, say that there has been no effect that we can see and, therefore, the future effect is going to be minimal.

As far as the causes of this one-half degree increase are concerned, do sci-

*entists in your field, really the climate scientists, have a settled conclusion
as to why that's occurred?*

No. I think right now everyone's looking at the sun as one reason,
but there are issues of the ocean, ocean circulation, ocean changes on
time scales of decades to centuries. And we don't understand that. We
don't understand the mechanism for the sun. There's still many surprises left.

Would you say, in general, that at this point the science is unsettled?

The science altogether is unsettled, but we know for sure that the
models that make the predictions into the future are exaggerating the
warmth.

Continued Climate Change

*Let's say everyone stopped emitting any greenhouse gas. All human green-
house gases were just halted. Do you think that it's still possible to have
global warming?*

Yes. If the causes of global warming are not owing to human activities, then the climate will continue on its course of change. It may be
solar, it may be related to the oceans, it may be internal to the Earth's
climate. So the fact that we stop emitting carbon dioxide will do
nothing to change the course of the climate. There's one interesting
related issue, which is carbon dioxide in the air in recent decades has
produced a tremendous agricultural boon. There have been estimates
of at least a 10% efficiency increase. So plants have been growing
quicker, better, greener. Crops have been growing better. This has
been for free, essentially. So cutting carbon dioxide means we lose
that increase in efficiency that we've gained.

*But back in 1100, 1200 we saw a rise in the temperature of the Earth,
even though, I guess we can assume there weren't a lot of greenhouse gases
being emitted by people in the Middle Ages.*

That's right, absolutely. In the 10th, 11th century, it looks to me
like the sun's energy output rose and that's really what caused the
warming back then. If you're a student of history, you'll know that
was a great time of expansion in Europe: town building, city building,
university building, church building, trade, because the climate was
really benign.

*Has anyone brought forth any evidence that says, "Dr. Baliunas says
there's a correlation between magnetic activity of the sun and the rise of
temperature on Earth, but this, that and the other disproves that"?*

I don't see how you can disprove the correlation. The next step is
for us to find the mechanism for that correlation. The correlation is
only the starting point. It may be that it's a coincidence that these
two things have changed together.

But that would be quite a coincidence?

It seems odd because we have some mechanisms that look like they
might explain it. We now have to prove that.

Trying to Predict the Weather

I've read a lot about how humans are going to be causing a dramatic warming. A [2001] summary of a UN report forecast possible floods and extreme weather and outbreaks of malaria—incredible predictions.

They're not credible, as the scientific report states. To get an estimate of what climate is going to be by region is not possible region by region. And you can't look at those outcomes like floods and storms. Models have no ability to see storm fronts, for example. So they can't predict storminess. It even brings up the point about how credible the average temperatures are, globally—those that are often quoted. Global averages are made out of region-by-region averages, which are admittedly incorrect—wrong in some cases by 11 degrees C over portions of the United States. Rainfall is wrong by 200% in some areas. So averaging out all of those mistakes can't possibly give you anything reliable, even in the global average.

We know how difficult it is to predict the weather for tomorrow; so, how are we going to predict the climate 100 years from now?

That's exactly the problem. Predicting the weather is done on a very small scale. We have to try to do that globally, but we can't do that because the computer power isn't available. We also don't have the knowledge of what changes the climate. So we have to make some assumptions and guesses. There are something like five million parameters that have to go into a good climate model, and it has to compute for a time longer than the age of the universe if we wanted to know something. So we can't. We have to make simplified assumptions. We know those assumptions are wrong. We know the outcome doesn't match up with reality.

THE INFLUENCE OF FRINGE SCIENCE ON GLOBAL WARMING POLICY

Katharine Mieszkowski

According to Katharine Mieszkowski, the fringe science espoused by those who refute the existence of global warming is having a disproportionate influence on federal climate policy. Although mainstream science has accepted the fact that global warming is occurring, Mieszkowski asserts, a handful of scientists backed by the energy industry claim that the phenomenon does not exist. These naysayers have been able to create the appearance that no scientific consensus on global warming has been reached, thus increasing public uncertainty about the potential threat of climate change, the author maintains. Furthermore, she continues, many conservative politicians—including President George W. Bush and his administration—have embraced the views of these skeptics in order to put off making any real strides toward addressing the global warming problem. Mieszkowski is a senior writer for Salon.com.

When the White House announced its 10-year strategic plan for its Climate Change Science Program [in] July [2003], the more than 300-page document could be summed up in two words: more research.

The plan's No. 1 priority is to study the ways that the climate varies naturally, as in, for example, the El Niño phenomenon. A secondary priority is to gather more information on human, or non-natural, impacts on the atmosphere. Whether caused by burning fossil fuels, cutting down forests or belching industrial pollution, man-made effects on climate can be "quantified only poorly at present," according to the plan. So, to "reduce uncertainty" more data collection is needed.

It's a research agenda that enshrines the suspicions of global warming skeptics into federal policy: "Looking at the executive summary, I'm generally pleased with it," says William O'Keefe from the George C. Marshall Institute, a think tank that's received hundreds of thousands of dollars of funding from ExxonMobil. "The reason that they've focused on research is not a way to slow down taking action,"

Katherine Mieszkowski, "The Triumph of Fringe Science," www.salon.com, August 7, 2003. Copyright © 2003 by the Salon Media Group. Reproduced by permission.

he says. "Most of what we think we know about the climate system and human impacts on it comes from computer models that are based on hypotheses. There is a terrible deficit of real scientific information where you actually go out and gather data."

While the White House preaches the need for more study, more than 2,000 scientists from across the globe—contributors to the U.N.'s Intergovernmental Panel on Climate Change—have been in agreement since 1995 that human activities are contributing to worldwide warming. The United States' own National Academy of Sciences reported in 2001 that some of the warming of the Earth's atmosphere over the last 50 years is caused by greenhouse gas emissions, such as carbon dioxide generated by the burning of fossil fuels.

A Political Stalling Tactic

Environmentalists see the White House research plan as just another stalling tactic to avoid regulating pollution to mitigate global warming. "Most climate scientists around the world will see this as fiddling while Rome burns," says Philip E. Clapp, president of the National Environmental Trust.

For years, industry-backed global warming naysayers have claimed that the rise in global temperatures is not a real problem, is not caused by humans, and if it is in fact happening at all, it's actually good for the world. The Marshall Institute, for instance, began making that case in 1989, when it released a report arguing that "cyclical variations in the intensity of the sun would offset any climate change associated with elevated greenhouse gases." The view that nature would save us from ourselves was refuted by the Intergovernmental Panel on Climate Change, but was still influential with the first President Bush's climate policy, according to the Union of Concerned Scientists.

Now, more than a decade later, the new Bush administration is continuing to codify the naysaying view of global warming skeptics into government policy, counter to the growing consensus of most of the world's climate scientists. Their frustration is palpable: While more research is always good, they say, no amount of further study will change the fact that humans are in fact contributing to the warming of the planet.

"Ludicrous," is how Raymond Bradley, the director of the University of Massachusetts Climate System Research Center in Amherst, Mass., characterized the plan at a meeting of some 1,000 climate scientists in late July [2003], reported on by the Associated Press. "Right now, we have good, strong scientific evidence supported by the vast majority of scientists who studied the problem to say we are facing a serious problem," he said.

Bradley charged that the White House is capitulating to "fringe science. . . . Politicians are always faced with making decisions in the face of uncertainty, but I think the uncertainty over this issue is relatively low."

It may be low among a preponderance of scientists who have spent their careers studying the problem, but their certainty isn't bending the ears of those who control the levers of power. The global warming skeptics, lavishly funded by precisely those corporations that have the most to fear from new regulations aimed at reducing emissions of greenhouse gases, have succeeded in perpetuating the notion that there's a genuine, ongoing scientific dispute as to the reality and causes of global warming. Fringe science is no longer on the periphery. Instead, it rules triumphant. Before the November 2002 election, a Republican strategy memo warned party leaders that they should soften their message on the environment, recasting "global warming" as the more palatable "climate change," a phrase that sounds closer to what happens when you board a plane in Anchorage and get off in Houston than it does to some scary global crisis.

The now infamous Luntz memo advised that "voters believe that there is no consensus about global warming within the scientific community. Should the public come to believe that the scientific issues are settled, their views about global warming will change accordingly. Therefore, you need to continue to make the lack of scientific certainty a primary issue in the debate. . . ."

Creating Uncertainty

Administration officials looking for data to back the uncertainty theory haven't had to look far for sources of information. According to Ross Gelbspan, author of *The Heat Is On*, an investigative expose documenting how corporate dollars influence the debate over global warming published back in the late '90s, there's a coal, auto and oil industry–funded cadre of professional skeptics and pundits that has been pushing the "uncertainty" line, with increasing success, for years.

The skeptics are sponsored by groups that include the Competitive Enterprise Institute, the Center for the Study of Carbon Dioxide and Global Change, the Greening Earth Society and the George C. Marshall Institute.

"They manufacture uncertainty," says Virginia Ashby Sharpe, director of the Integrity in Science project at the Center for Science in the Public Interest.

Uncertainty about global warming is a view the White House unambiguously supports. [In] September [2002], a section on global warming in the annual federal pollution report from the Environmental Protection Agency was simply deleted, with White House approval. But it's not just inside the administration that these uncertainties find a receptive audience.

In late July [2003], as senators debated the energy bill, Sen. James M. Inhofe, R-Okla., made a speech in the Senate calling for "sound science" to be the source of decision-making about global warming while simultaneously asserting: "With all the hysteria, all the fear, all the phony science, could it be that manmade global warming is the greatest hoax ever perpetrated on the American people? I believe it is."

In his lengthy talk, Sen. Inhofe said: "After studying the issue over the last several years, I believe the balance of the evidence offers strong proof that natural variability, not manmade, is the overwhelming factor influencing climate, and that manmade gases are virtually irrelevant." To support this point of view, he cited, among other sources, a recent paper titled "Reconstructing Climatic and Environmental Changes of the Past 1,000 Years: A Reappraisal" which concluded that the earth was actually warmer during the Middle Ages than it is now.

Corporate Influence

Inhofe called the paper "the most comprehensive study of its kind in history," but failed to note that the research was underwritten by the American Petroleum Institute, an energy industry trade group, and that four of the five coauthors of the study have affiliations with groups backed by oil, gas or coal money.

Astrophysicist Sallie Baliunas and physicist Willie Soon, both scientists at the Harvard-Smithsonian Center for Astrophysics, are also "senior scientists" at the ExxonMobil-backed Marshall Institute.

The father and son team of Sherwood and Craig Idso hail from the Center for the Study of Carbon Dioxide and Global Change in Tempe, Ariz., which has also received money from ExxonMobil. In the early '90s, Dr. Sherwood Idso narrated the video "The Greening of Planet Earth," which was funded by $250,000 from the Western Fuels Association, a coal-industry association, and according to Gelbspan, predicted that global warming will cause increased crop yields. In other words, global warming is good for us.

Sen. Inhofe complained in the Senate about the reporting of these energy-industry affiliations when the study came out: "Unfortunately, some of the media could not resist playing politics of personal destruction," he said. The senator himself has received some $543,269 in campaign contributions from energy and natural resources companies and, PACs [political action committees], more than twice as much as from any other category.

And, as reported in the *Wall Street Journal*, Hans von Storch, the editor of *Climate Research*, the journal in which "A Reappraisal" was published, recently resigned, along with two other top editors, to protest "irregularities" in the editorial process that allowed the paper to be published. But the fact that the paper itself is being widely criticized hasn't hampered its influence on policy.

Journalistic Balance

Politicians in the White House and Congress, amply lubricated by energy money, don't deserve all the blame for the ascendancy of the global warming uncertainty principle. Part of the problem lies with journalists, says Gelbspan, a former reporter and editor himself.

Gelbspan criticizes reporters for constantly turning to energy industry–funded organizations for a "balancing" quote when writing about climate change. "This whole thing about journalistic balance: it's relevant when they're doing a story based on opinions, like abortion, but when it's a story based on fact there is no issue of balance involved at all," he says. "I think that the fossil fuel public relations people are really exploiting this misguided notion of journalistic balance, and the skeptics are taking advantage of it."

Gelbspan's critique is echoed by other representatives of the conservation movement.

"You'll find that their science fellows or adjunct board members or advisors or council of poohbahs always falls back to this handful of 'scientists' in this other category of people who have now made a living for the past five or 10 years on being skeptics on climate change," says Kert Davies, a research director at Greenpeace who has spent years tracking the funding of global warming skeptics. "If anybody wants a balanced story on climate, these knuckleheads get quoted, although we would say it doesn't reflect the balance of scientists."

While most climate scientists agree that the most general issues about global warming are settled—Principally, is global warming happening? Yes. And do human activities have a role in it? Yes.—there are unanswered questions that help the skeptics spread doubt.

"The only kind of skepticism that I would accept from a colleague would be the uncertainty in just how much of a role humans have versus other possible causes," says Michael E. Mann, a paleoclimatologist and professor at the University of Virginia, whose research on warming has been embraced by the Intergovernmental Panel on Climate Change. But what there isn't any lingering doubt about in the scientific community, says Mann, is that humans have played a role in the warming that's occurred in the last century.

In Search of Funding

The skeptics also play their own funding card when arguing that scientists have every reason to perpetuate the idea that there's a massive crisis building. Myron Ebell, the director of global warming policy at the Competitive Enterprise Institute, a conservative think tank that's received funding from ExxonMobil, the Ford Motor Company Foundation, General Motors Foundation, Texaco Inc. Foundation and others, claims that there are plenty of scientists who believe that this whole global warming crisis is "essentially bunkem," but "they won't speak up," since there's a gravy-train of federal money going to fund research projects in this area.

He casts the great global warming scare as a phony crisis manufactured by a bunch of chicken-little eggheads in search of funding for their pet research projects: "You've got to make noise now in order to get funding through Congress or the bureaucracy. If it's not some kind of crisis that the public cares about, it's not going to get funding," says Ebell, imagining the thought processes inside the mind of a money-hungry scientist brain: "'I've got to get people to notice me! I've got to have a crisis! Or, I'm not going to get any money, or not very much money.'"

The Marshall Institute's O'Keefe echoes that view. "I'm not saying that people are being dishonest," says O'Keefe. "I'm saying the system creates incentives for work that promotes more funding. 'If you give me more money I'll be able to show that.'" He blames the lingering influence of Al Gore for the climate gravy train: "In the early '90s, it was absolutely clear that the vice president of the U.S. had made a decision that there was a serious problem, and people who wanted to get government funding had to be generally consistent with the Gore view of global warming."

But now the research dollars are flowing under the Bush Administration for climate study, like the $103 million for the new Climate Science plan, precisely because of the uncertainty around global warming that groups such as the Marshall Institute have helped promote.

Another fact of climate science that helps the skeptics make their case is the reliance upon computer models for conducting research. Ebell scoffs at the climate models that researchers use to try to predict how much average temperatures will increase in coming decades: "As long as they put in junk assumptions, you're going to get junk out of the models." What we need, he says, is "more basic research to know what the problem is, and what it might develop into."

But Mann says that the computer models are a way of formalizing the questions that climate scientists are trying to test so that assumptions can be changed, verified and cross-validated. He points out that the skeptics who cast blanket doubt on such models want their own intuitive assumptions about climate studies to be trusted instead: "The irony often is that they will reject the models that we try to use to understand physical systems. They'll reject them in exchange for their own kind of unconstrained idea."

The Unending Debate

But beyond the real scientific questions that are still open, skeptics are able to take ample advantage of the larger fact that scientific debate is hardly ever definitively closed, once and for all.

"Science is always based on information that you have right now," says Sharpe from the Center for the Science in the Public Interest. "So, you can hardly ever say in an unqualified way that a debate has been definitively closed. Most scientific inquiry is based on the idea that it's always ongoing. The inquiry is always open."

"That is no reason for inaction in the face of strong evidence of significant harm. When the oil industry claims that 'the science is uncertain' on global warming and that voters should be made to believe that there is 'no consensus,' it is saying that we should not act on the basis of current evidence—which unanimously links global warming with human activities—except for those studies and opinions paid for by the industry."

Ironically, [in July 2003] there was evidence of an instance in which concerted action based on the best available science at the time paid dividends on an environmental issue. The destruction of the ozone layer has apparently slowed, thanks to the phasing out of chlorofluorocarbons that began with the Montreal Protocol in 1989.

"We enacted the Montreal Protocol to reduce the release of chlorofluorocarbons into the atmosphere with far less consensus than we've got on this issue. A third less science than this, and much less consensus," says Matthew Follett, the co-founder of the Green House Network, a grass-roots effort against global warming.

But maybe it's naive to think that scientific consensus alone would force the U.S. to ratify the Kyoto Protocol, as it did the Montreal Protocol. With a raft of skeptics, backed by funding from the energy biz—the largest industry in the world—and politicians eager to embrace their skeptical views, there's always going to be more than enough "uncertainty" to put off doing anything until more data is available.

MEDIA MISREPRESENTATION OF GLOBAL WARMING STUDIES

Mark LaRochelle and Peter Spencer

Journalists often misinterpret or misreport the results of scientific research concerning global warming, Mark LaRochelle and Peter Spencer contend in the following article. The authors look specifically at news reports about studies released by the Intergovernmental Panel on Climate Change (IPCC) and the National Research Council (NRC) in 2001. According to LaRochelle and Spencer, numerous magazines and newspapers stated that these studies had reached the conclusion that global warming was real, getting worse, and due largely to human activity. In fact, the authors maintain, the IPCC and the NRC both cautioned that the studies' findings were tentative, needed careful interpretation, and should not be oversimplified by the media. This incident is a typical example of the press's tendency to exaggerate the extent of the global warming phenomenon, they conclude. LaRochelle is an associate editor for the National Journalism Center. Spencer is the former editor of *Consumers' Research Magazine* and has written for the *Encyclopedia Britannica* and the *Washington Post*.

For more than a decade now, consumers have been confronted with frequent warnings that our carbon-dioxide-producing, modern way of life contributes to global warming, and thus is setting up the world for climatic catastrophe—unless we do something to reverse course soon.

Nothing new here, but . . . the warnings have taken on a heightened sense of urgency following reports that scientific authorities have answered some key questions about the underlying science behind global-warming estimates. This increased certainty, we have been led to believe, strengthens the case for "action" on global warming, which typically involves instituting policies to meet the goals of the Kyoto global warming treaty, signed by the Clinton Administration in 1997.

Whether such efforts would do any good is another issue entirely. At this point, judgment about whether even to take action first requires some understanding of the underlying knowledge about cli-

Mark LaRochelle and Peter Spencer, "Scientists Remain Uncertain: 'Global Warming' Science: Fact vs. Fiction," *Consumers' Research Magazine*, vol. 84, July 2001, p. 10. Copyright © 2001 by Consumers' Research, Inc. Reproduced by permission.

mate change. And, as closer scrutiny of the relevant data reveals, the underlying facts on this front are quite the opposite of what has been popularly portrayed.

The End of the Global Warming Debate?

As trumpeted by the popular media, our new alleged certainty about the effects and causes of global warming stem from two scientific studies: The first, drawn from a lengthy compendium of climate-change data put together by the United Nations' Intergovernmental Panel on Climate Change (IPCC), was released [in the winter of 2001]. The second, a follow-up study on the same subject, [was] released [in June 2001] by the National Research Council (NRC) of the National Academy of Sciences.

In both cases, publicity about these reports suggested, in so many words, that the debate about "global warming" was over. Commenting on the original IPCC study, for instance, *Time* magazine asserted: "Scientists no longer doubt that global warming is happening, and almost nobody questions the fact that humans are at least partly responsible."

"A decade ago, the idea that the planet was warming up as a result of human activity was largely theoretical," the newsmagazine explained [in] April [2001]. ". . . Not anymore. As an authoritative report issued a few weeks ago by the [IPCC] makes plain, the trend toward a warmer world has unquestionably begun."

U.S. News and World Report, among other news outlets, offered a similar take on the IPCC study, calling it "the most definitive—and scary—report yet, declaring that global warming is not only real but man-made."

Yet the study in question was not all that it was made out to be. The publication, a mere 20-page "Summary for Policymakers" based on a . . . 3,000-page report, hardly represented an authoritative picture of IPCC science, say climate researchers familiar with the project.

Interpreting Scientific Research

In fact, these researchers say, the full report itself is heavily nuanced, containing numerous qualifications, provisos and cautions about the proper interpretation of the data—as is fairly typical of scientific studies relying on many and varied sources. Most of this nuance was simply omitted in the summary, which came across as categorical and definite, thus giving rise to the scary stories.

It was precisely because of this discrepancy that the second study was commissioned—in effect, a study of a study. Because of serious questions about the reliability of the IPCC summary, in May [2001] the White House asked the National Research Council to identify "the areas in the science of climate change where there are the greatest certainties and uncertainties," and to comment in particular on the quality of science represented in the IPCC summary that had been making so many headlines.

And, ironically, the same thing happened all over again. Once more, the report in question stressed nuance and uncertainty. And once more the media stories took their cues from the boiled-down treatment available in the report's summary.

Thus, *The New York Times* reported that NRC analysis "reaffirmed the mainstream scientific view that the earth's atmosphere was getting warmer and that human activity was largely responsible." And CNN reported that the report represented "a unanimous decision that global warming is real, is getting worse, and is due to man. There is no wiggle room."

Such characterizations could not have been more misleading. In very explicit terms, for instance, the NRC warned that over-simplifying the state of knowledge could mislead the public to believe the science was "settled." This, it noted, happened with the IPCC, because details of the scientific uncertainties were omitted from its summary.

A Degree of Skepticism

A more accurate reading of the state of science, the NRC reported, indicates that researchers simply cannot predict with any assurance whether the earth will in fact heat up to a dangerous extent over the next century or whether man's impact will make a significant mark, one way or the other. Moreover, the NRC emphasized that recognition of what scientists don't know here is central to the debates about policy ventures. As the report noted, "thorough understanding of the uncertainties is essential to the development of good policy decisions."

In essence, the message of the NRC panel was that sound science should inform policy decisions and that this requires a degree of skepticism to be sure of the facts: "The most valuable contribution U.S. scientists can make is to continually question basic assumptions and conclusions, promote clear and careful appraisal and presentation of the uncertainties about climate change . . . and work toward a significant improvement in the ability to project the future." It is difficult to square this point-of-view with the message of settled science portrayed in news reports.

So just what does mainstream science know about global warming? By way of overview, Massachusetts Institute of Technology Professor Richard S. Lindzen, one of the NRC panelists (and a lead author in the . . . IPCC report), provides a helpful precis:

"Our primary conclusion was that despite some knowledge and agreement, the science is by no means settled. We are quite confident (1) that global mean temperature is about 0.5 degrees Celsius higher than it was a century ago; (2) that atmospheric levels of carbon dioxide have risen over the past two centuries; and (3) that carbon dioxide is a greenhouse gas whose increase is likely to warm the earth (one of many, the most important being water vapor and clouds). But—and I cannot stress this enough—we are not in a position to confidently attribute past climate change to carbon dioxide or to forecast what the climate will be in the future."

"That is to say," Lindzen adds, "contrary to media impressions, agreement with the three basic statements tells us almost nothing relevant to policy discussions."

What Do Scientists Need to Know?

Given the large gaps in knowledge, the NRC's discussion does indicate research areas to watch closely. In general, scientists need more solid information in three areas: the historical climate record, the man-made impact on the climate, and the computer models used to predict future trends.

Historical Climate Record. Despite general agreement that the world has warmed slightly over the past 100 years or so, there remains considerable room for improving the accuracy—and assurance—of this asserted warming. At this point, results of measured warming, the NRC notes, "are somewhat equivocal."

Consider the surface temperature record—as opposed to satellite and weather-balloon temperature measurements—which serves as the principle basis for official scientific statements about a warming planet. The surface record is compiled from two very different sources: a land record of air temperatures at weather stations, and an ocean record of water temperatures. Between various biases identified in each, the combined surface record may substantially overestimate 20th century warming, say some scientists connected with the IPCC report. "The surface data are less than perfect, to put it mildly," says Roy Spencer, senior scientist for climate studies at NASA's Marshall Space Flight Center, who provided the IPCC's satellite data.

The land record, for instance, is notoriously spotty, and, as the IPCC points out, biased by effects that require substantial correction. Explains Spencer: "Thermometers cover less than half of the earth's surface and are unevenly distributed, with more measurements being taken in the northern hemisphere than in the southern hemisphere. On land, temperature readings have to be corrected for the 'heat island' effect, a local warming that occurs over time as cities spread outward."

The ocean record has uncertainties of its own. Changes in the way ocean temperatures have been measured, the gradual addition of tropical buoys, and the growing discrepancy between ocean and air temperatures have each exercised an upward bias.

"Until the 1940s, ships would measure sea surface temperatures by dropping a thermometer into a bucket of sea water," explains Spencer. "Today sea water temperatures are measured by thermometers affixed to buoys, or in the intake ports of ships." He adds: "Recently, the addition of ocean buoy measurements in the tropical east Pacific and their role in recording a possible false warming has come under investigation. There is also evidence that air temperatures taken just above the ocean surface have not risen nearly as fast as sea water temperatures, and it is sea water temperatures that have, up until now, been included in global temperature estimates."

Similar uncertainties turn up in the satellite and weather balloon data used by the IPCC. For example, since global observations began in 1958, balloons have recorded a warming of approximately 0.05 degrees C (plus or minus 0.10 degrees) per decade. These data, however, are controversial. "The uncertainties are very large," says Julian Wang of NOAA's [the National Oceanic and Atmospheric Administration] Air Resources Laboratory, who together with James Angell, published the balloon data used by the IPCC. "The measurement error is larger than the trend," says Wang. That means "the trend is effectively zero, and could be negative," he told *Consumers' Research*. "The natural variability is also larger than the trend," he added, "so the observed trend could be entirely natural."

In point of fact, the surface, balloon, and satellite temperature records all contain sufficient margins of error to wipe out any estimated trend in warming over the past century.

Man's Impact on Climate Change. News reports highlight statements that acknowledge warming over the past century "is unlikely to be entirely natural in origin," in the words of the IPCC summary, in a passage played up widely in the press. But the NRC also warns that "a causal linkage between the buildup of greenhouse gases in the atmosphere and the observed climate change during the 20th century cannot be unequivocally established."

"Whether [the observed warming] is consistent with the change that would be expected in response to human activities is dependent upon what assumptions one makes," the NRC concluded.

The scientific question is whether that human contribution is detectable given the range of natural variability. The NRC observes that "there is considerable uncertainty in current understanding of how the climate system varies naturally." It adds, "uncertainty remains because of . . . the level of natural variability in the climate system on time scales of decades to centuries." The report concludes, "The range of natural climate variability is known to be quite large (in excess of several degrees Celsius) on local and regional spatial scales over periods as short as a decade."

Even if the natural variability were known, the observed warming would likely be within that range. To discern the human impact on climate, it would also be necessary to know how various emissions interact with the atmosphere. But according to the NRC, "there is considerable uncertainty in current understanding of how the climate system reacts . . . to emissions of greenhouse gases."

Problems with Historical Climate Models

Computer Models. Given such wide natural variability, how does the IPCC distinguish the human contribution to climate? According to its summary report, it used computer models to estimate what the 20th century temperature trend would have been in the absence of humans, then attributed any discrepancy between the models' predictions and recorded temperatures to greenhouse gas emissions.

"Some recent models produce satisfactory simulations of current climate," says the summary. Yet the NRC found that "climate models are imperfect. Their simulation skill is limited by uncertainties in their formulation, the limited size of their calculations, and the difficulty of interpreting their answers that exhibit almost as much complexity as in nature."

It added: "Uncertainty remains because of . . . the questionable ability of models to accurately simulate natural variability on . . . long time scales [of decades to centuries]."

But if the accuracy of the models is questionable, how do we know that the discrepancy between the models' predictions and observed temperatures lies with problems in the atmosphere, and not in the models?

The NRC notes that models "show forced responses of the global-mean temperature that corresponds roughly with its measured history over the past century, though this requires model adjustments." How useful are predictions made by a model that requires such "adjustments" in order to correspond "roughly" with history? The NRC diplomatically avoids pointing out that such "adjustment" is normally called "fudging."

The scientific method requires testing any model against real-world data to determine the model's predictive accuracy. As the NRC put it, "the greater the sophistication and complexity of an atmospheric model, the greater the need for detailed, multiple measurements, which test whether the model continues to mimic observational reality."

In fact, the models have been dismal at modeling historical climate—estimating for the 20th century, for example, nearly twice the warming actually observed. As the NRC report delicately phrases the problem, "The warming that has been estimated to have occurred in response to the buildup of greenhouse gases in the atmosphere is somewhat greater than the observed warming."

When run forward from historical data, the models have drastically overestimated regional temperature over the 20th century, and missed even vast historic global climate changes such as ice ages. Models, as the NRC notes, can "not yet provide for continuous evolution over longer intervals (transitions between ice ages)."

Future Model Predictions. Given the uncertainty in the temperature record and of the human contribution, it is hard to see how models can accurately predict future warming. To do so, they would not only have to model natural variability, historical climate, and current atmospheric temperatures accurately—but also the interaction of various as yet poorly understood factors, such as aerosol emissions and, even more important, clouds.

Moreover, if current trends continue, the IPCC's predicted future greenhouse gas emissions are likely to prove to be overestimates. "The increase of global fossil fuel carbon dioxide emissions in the past decade has averaged 0.6% per year, which is somewhat below the range of IPCC scenarios," says the NRC. More important, notes the report, unforeseeable "technological capabilities . . . may allow reduction of greenhouse gas emissions by 2100."

Potential Blunders

In sum, a false impression of certainty, warned the NRC, could lead the public to serious blunders: "Without an understanding of the sources and degree of uncertainty, decision-makers could fail to define the best ways to deal with the serious issue of global warming."

The conventional wisdom that the . . . IPCC summary and NRC study herald a new certainty about global warming is simply false. A reading of these surveys imparts a growing awareness of the vast uncertainties that surround our meager understanding of the earth, and man's role on it—for good or ill.

CHAPTER 2

THE CONSEQUENCES OF GLOBAL WARMING

THE WORLDWIDE EFFECTS OF GLOBAL WARMING

Mark Lynas

Journalist and environmental activist Mark Lynas spent three years traveling around the world to research the impact of global warming for his book *High Tide: News from a Warming World*. In the following selection, he describes the climate changes he observed during his journey—from Alaska, where unusually warm temperatures and melting ice are destroying native Alaskans' villages and their traditional way of life, to China, where droughts and dust storms are turning parts of the country into a desert. Lynas asserts that signs of global warming are dramatically apparent all over the planet and are already having a direct effect on people's lives. Furthermore, Lynas believes that these changes are only the beginning; if nothing is done to stop global warming, he warns, the earth will experience unimaginable climate catastrophes.

Hardly anyone realises it, but the debate about climate change is over. Scientists around the world have now amassed an unassailable body of evidence to support the conclusion that a warming of our planet— caused principally by greenhouse gas emissions from burning fossil fuel—is under way.

The dwindling band of climate "sceptics", a rag-tag bunch of oil and coal industry frontmen, retired professors and semi-deranged obsessives, is now on the defensive. Although names such as Fred Singer, Philip Stott and Bjorn Lomborg still appear from time to time in the popular press [in England] and in the United States, their views are notable by their absence from the expert literature.

Meanwhile the world as we once knew it is beginning to unravel. The signs are everywhere, even in Britain. Horse chestnut, oak and ash trees are coming into leaf more than a week earlier than two decades ago. The growing season now lasts almost all year round: in 2000 there were just 39 official days of winter.

Destructive winter floods are part of this warming trend, while in lowland England snow has become a thing of the past. Where I live in Oxford, six out of the past ten winters have been completely snow-

Mark Lynas, "It's Later than You Think," *New Statesman*, vol. 132, June 30, 2003, pp. 16–17. Copyright © 2003 by New Statesman, Ltd. Reproduced by permission.

less—something that happened only twice during the whole 30-year period between 1960 and 1990. The rate of warming has now become so rapid that it is equivalent to your garden moving south by 20 metres every single day.

Change Across Five Continents

In other parts of the world, the signs of global warming are more dramatic. . . . Researching a book on the subject, I have witnessed major climate-driven changes across five continents, changes that are leaving millions homeless, destitute and in danger.

In Alaska I spent a week in the Eskimo village of Shishmaref, on the state's remote western coast, just 70 miles from the eastern coast of Russia. While the midnight sun shone outside, I listened as the village elder, Clifford Weyiouanna, told me how the sea, which used to freeze in October, was now ice-free until Christmas. And even when the sea ice does eventually form, he explained, it is so thin that it is dangerous to walk and hunt on. The changing seasons are also affecting the animals: seals and walruses—still crucial elements of the Eskimo diet—are migrating earlier and are almost impossible to catch. The whole village caught only one walrus [in 2002] after covering thousands of miles by boat.

Shishmaref lives in perpetual fear. The cliffs on which the 600-strong community sits are thawing, and during the last big storm 50 feet of ground was lost overnight. People battled 90 mph winds to save their houses from the crashing waves.

I stood on the shoreline [in 2002] with Robert Iyatunguk, the co-ordinator of the Shishmaref Erosion Coalition, looking up at a house left hanging over the clifftop. "The wind is getting stronger, the water is getting higher, and it's noticeable to everybody in town," he told me. "It just kind of scares you inside your body and makes you wonder exactly when the big one is going to hit." In July 2002 the residents voted to abandon the site altogether—a narrow barrier island that has been continuously occupied by Eskimos for centuries—and move elsewhere.

In Fairbanks, Alaska's main town in the interior, everyone talks about warming. The manager of the hostel where I stayed, a keen hunter, told me how ducks had been swimming on the river in December (it's supposed to freeze over in autumn), how bears had become so confused they didn't know whether to hibernate or stay awake, and that winter temperatures, which used to plummet to 40 degrees below zero, now barely touched 25 below.

All around the town, roads are buckling and houses sagging as the permafrost underneath them thaws. In one house, the occupants, a cleaning lady and her daughter, showed me that to walk across the kitchen meant going uphill (the house was tilting sideways) and how shelves had to be rebalanced with bits of wood to stop everything from falling off. Other dwellings have been abandoned. New ones are built on adjustable stilts.

Droughts in China

Scientists have long predicted that global warming will lead in some places to intense flooding and drought. When I visited China in April [2002], the country's northern provinces were in the grip of the worst drought in more than a century. Entire lakes had dried up, and in many places sand dunes were advancing across the farmers' fields.

One lakeside village in Gansu Province, just off the old Silk Road, was abandoned after the waters dried up—apart from one woman, who lives amid the ruins with a few chickens and a cow for company. "Of course I'm lonely!" she cried in answer to my rather insensitive question. "Can you imagine how boring this life is? I can't move; I can do nothing. I have no relatives, no friends and no money." She was tormented by memories of how it had once been, when neighbours had chatted and swapped stories late into the evenings, before the place became a ghost town.

Minutes after I had left, a dust storm blew in. These storms are getting more frequent, and even Beijing is now hit repeatedly every spring. During an earlier visit to a remote village in eastern Inner Mongolia, not far from the ruins of Kubla Khan's fabled Xanadu, I experienced an even stronger storm. Day was turned into night as a blizzard of sand and dust scoured the mud-brick buildings. I cowered inside one house with a Mongolian peasant family, sharing rice wine and listening to tales of how the grass had once grown waist-high on the surrounding plains. Now the land is little more than arid desert, thanks to persistent drought and overgrazing. The storm raged for hours. When it eased in the late afternoon and the sun appeared again, the village cockerels crowed, thinking that morning had come early.

Threatened Water Supplies

The drought in north-west China is partly caused by shrinking run-off from nearby mountains, which because of the rising temperatures are now capped with less snow and ice than before. Glacier shrinkage is a phenomenon repeated across the world's mountain ranges, and I also saw it at first hand in Peru, standing dizzy with altitude sickness in the high Andes 5,200 metres above the capital, Lima, where one of the main water-supplying glaciers has shrunk by more than a kilometre during the past century.

A senior manager of Lima's water authority told me later how melting ice is now a critical threat to future freshwater supplies: this city of seven million is the world's second-largest desert metropolis after Cairo, and the mountains supply all its water through coastal rivers that pour down from the ice fields far above. It is the snows that keep the rivers running all year round—once the glaciers are gone, the rivers will flow only in the wet season. The same problem afflicts the Indian subcontinent: overwhelmingly dependent on the mighty Ganges, Indus and Brahmaputra rivers that flow from the Himalayas, hundreds of millions of people will suffer water shortages as their source glaciers decline over the coming century.

Unless alternative water supplies can be secured, Lima will be left depopulated, its people scattered as environmental refugees. This is a category already familiar to the residents of Tuvalu, a group of nine coral atolls in the middle of the Pacific. Tuvalu, together with Kiribati, the Maldives and many other island nations, has made its plight well known to the world community, and an evacuation plan—shifting 75 people each year to New Zealand—is already under way.

I saw at first hand how the islands are already affected by the rising sea level, paddling in knee-deep floodwaters during [2002's] spring tides, which submerged much of Funafuti and almost surrounded the airstrip. Later that same evening the country's first post-independence prime minister, Toaripi Lauti, told me of his shock at finding his own crop of pulaka (a root vegetable like taro, grown in sunken pits) dying from saltwater intrusion. He recalled how everyone had awoken one morning a few years previously to find that one of the islets on the atoll's rim had disappeared from the horizon, washed over by the waves, its coconut trees smashed and destroyed by the rising sea.

Stopping Climate Catastrophe

However severe these unfolding climate-change impacts seem, they are—like the canary in the coal mine—just the first whispers of the holocaust that lies ahead if nothing is done to reduce greenhouse gas emissions. Scientists meeting under the banner of the UN-sponsored Intergovernmental Panel on Climate Change (IPCC) have predicted a warming during [the twenty-first] century alone of up to six degrees Celsius, which would take the earth into dangerous uncharted waters. [In June 2003], scientists at the UK's Hadley Centre reported that the warming might be even greater because of the complexities of the carbon cycle.

The IPCC's worst-case forecast of six degrees could prove almost unimaginably catastrophic. It took only six degrees of warming to spark the end-Permian mass extinction 251 million years ago, the worst crisis ever to hit life on earth, which led to the deaths of 95 per cent of all species alive at the time.

If humanity is to avoid a similar fate, global greenhouse gas emissions need to be brought down to between 60 and 80 per cent below current levels—precisely the reverse of emissions forecasts recently produced by the International Energy Agency. A good start would be the ratification and speedy implementation of the Kyoto Protocol, which should be superseded after the following decade by the "contraction and convergence" model proposed by the Global Commons Institute in London, allocating equal per-person emissions rights among all the world's nations.

In the meantime, a network of campaigning groups is currently mobilising under the banner of "No new oil", demanding an end to the exploration and development of new fossil fuel reserves, on the basis that current reserves alone include enough oil, coal and gas utterly to destabilise the world's climate. Searching for more is just as illogical as it is wasteful.

Avoiding dangerous climate change and other large-scale environmental crises will need to become the key organising principle around which societies evolve. All the signs are that few in power realise this—least of all the current US administration, which has committed itself to a policy of wanton destructiveness, with control and exploitation of oil supplies a central theme.

We must abandon the old mindset that demands an oil-based economy, not just because it sparks wars and terrorism, but because the future of life on earth depends on leaving it behind.

GLOBAL WARMING'S IMPACT ON WEATHER PATTERNS

Gabrielle Walker

Global warming may be affecting weather patterns worldwide, science writer Gabrielle Walker explains in the following selection. Scientists have noticed that catastrophic weather events such as storms and floods seem to be increasing in frequency and intensity, she writes, and they are investigating whether global warming is contributing to this phenomenon. While researchers have yet to come to a conclusion on whether global warming is causing more severe and unpredictable weather, the author reports, weather patterns are undeniably changing, and many experts believe this trend will worsen as the earth's temperature continues to rise. In addition, Walker notes, rising sea levels caused by the increase in global temperatures may wreak more havoc on weather patterns in the future. Walker is a consultant for *New Scientist* magazine and the author of the book *Snowball Earth*.

What's with the weather? An unruly beast at the best of times, it now seems to be lurching out of control. There are wildfires raging across the western US. India is reeling from floods . . . that left hundreds dead and millions homeless. Then there's the blistering heatwave in Greece, a bizarre contrast with Yorkshire's recent spectacular hailstorm, which left the streets of Hull looking for all the world as if it had snowed in August.

Open any newspaper or flick on the television and you'll find the same questions. What have we done? Is global warming upon us? Are we finally seeing the effects of our rash experiment with the world's climate?

They're hard questions to answer, not least because extreme weather has always been with us. "You can't say we had a flood in Mozambique and another in India and that must be down to global warming," says David Easterling, principal scientist at the National Climate Data Center (NCDC) in Asheville, North Carolina. "Even if [CO_2] levels hadn't changed in the 20th century, we would still see these events happen. You're going to have extremes in climate somewhere every year. The real question is: are we going to see a lot more of these in the future?"

To find out, researchers around the world are scouring records of temperature, wind and rain, trying to spot the patterns that will tell them whether things really are changing. Though they're still figuring out the details, one thing's for sure: even if the recent weather tantrums turn out to be nothing particularly new, the signs are that there's much worse to come.

The Effects of Warmer Temperatures

Of all the changes researchers are watching for, warming is the easiest to spot. Reliable temperature records stretch back to the mid-19th century. Before that, the data are more sparse, but there is evidence from ice cores, corals, old documents and tree rings of temperatures going back a thousand years or more. Thanks to these records, there's no longer serious argument about whether the Earth is heating up. The past century has seen average global temperature increase by more than half a degree, with the majority of that warming piled up in the latter half. The seven warmest years on record occurred in the 1990s, and 1998 was the hottest of all. "It was the warmest year in the warmest decade in the warmest century in the millennium," says Phil Jones, joint director of the University of East Anglia's Climatic Research Unit in Norwich [England].

The warming has made its mark. Around the world, there are fewer days when the temperature drops below freezing, and minimum temperatures everywhere are creeping upwards. All this seems very gentle, though, and it might even be nice. "Some people might like the effects of global warming," says Chris Folland of Britain's Meteorological Office in Bracknell. "It makes your holidays better." But it won't be all balmy summer evenings and mild winter days. There's a sinister side to warming as well.

Take the effect it could have on storms, for instance. Higher temperatures mean that more water evaporates from the Earth's surface. That could help crank up the heat engine that drives the weather. "Water vapour is a great energy source," says Catherine Senior, also from the Met Office, who has been studying the likely effects of global warming on storms in middle latitudes, away from the tropics and poles. By evaporating more water, she says, you're sucking energy out of the oceans and dumping it into the atmosphere where it's free to do its worst.

It's not quite that clear-cut, though. For middle latitudes at least, there's a competing effect stemming from global warming that could tend to quieten storms rather than stir them up. Researchers believe that the poles will warm more than the tropics because when you melt white ice at the poles, the darker land or water beneath soaks up more sunlight. The temperature difference between the tropics and poles is a great driver for creating storms, so reducing the temperature gradient ought to make storms less likely.

According to Senior's model, water vapour wins this climatic tug of war. [In 1998] she published results of a computer model suggesting that global warming will intensify mid-latitude storms, such as the one that battered southern England in October 1987. Other models come up with different answers, but that's because nobody's sure how these effects will play out. "It's not well understood what causes storms to form and deepen, and what path they take in today's climate," she says. "So trying to understand what might happen under climate change is even more difficult."

Increasing Storminess

Although not everyone agrees with the results of Senior's model, there are signs that we are already experiencing more formidable storms, in the North Atlantic at least. Ulrich Cubasch from the German Institute for Climate Research in Hamburg has found that in the past 20 years, mid-Atlantic depressions have become deeper—and the storms they cause more intense.

Even that may not be the effect of global warming, though. According to Folland, it could be down to a perfectly natural phenomenon known as the North Atlantic Oscillation [NAO]. This is in essence a climate cycle driven by the difference in pressure between the low that hovers over Iceland and the high over the Azores. If both are at their extremes, the NAO is said to be in its strong phase, and the gradient sets up fierce storms and westerly winds which drag the storms onto land. If the pressures are more equal, there are fewer storms, and easterly winds blowing off Europe prevent many of them from making landfall. Right now, the NAO is in its strong phase. It was also strong in the early 20th century, and Europe experienced more storms then as well. Folland also points out, though, that global warming could interfere with the NAO and cause more storminess in the next few decades.

When it comes to tropical storms, the picture is less ambiguous. It could be just a matter of time before the vicious hurricanes and cyclones that already hit the headlines start picking up energy from global warming and wreak still more havoc. As yet, global climate models are too coarse to resolve hurricanes, but hurricane researcher Kerry Emanuel from the Massachusetts Institute of Technology has found another way to tell what the future is likely to hold.

Hurricanes exist because of differences in temperature between the tropical ocean and atmosphere. Not all storms reach the maximum intensity that this temperature difference can produce. They may be held in check by factors like how long they persist and how much they stir up the ocean, bringing up cooler water to dampen their fervour. But weather scientists observing a particular storm can easily calculate how close it has come to achieving its full potential.

Equal Opportunities for Storms

In April [2000], Emanuel and his colleagues published a study of hurricane records from around the world going back 50 years. They looked at different parts of the world, different seasons and different time frames. To their astonishment they always saw a uniform pattern: each storm had the same chance of reaching any intensity you care to name, up to the maximum. There's no particular speed or proportion of the maximum that is more probable than any other. "Take a cyclone out in the Atlantic that's just developed, and there's an equal probability that it will get to 70 mph, 90 mph, 120 mph. It's true wherever you look," he says.

This gives climate prediction "a big leg up", says Emanuel. All you have to predict is the maximum intensity. In a warmer world, the maximum intensity for hurricanes will be greater everywhere. And if you raise the maximum possible intensity, Emanuel's research suggests that tropical storms will become more severe. "Lifting the tide lifts all the boats," he says.

Are there signs that this is happening? Well, not yet. Sure, tropical storms have been more catastrophic in recent years—in both human and economic cost. Hurricane Mitch, for instance, tore through Nicaragua and Honduras in 1998, causing more than 9000 deaths. But it wasn't a particularly severe storm. It just landed in a very unfortunate place. And the big bucks that insurance companies are shelling out for the eastern seaboard of the US owe more to increased development on the coast than they do to increased storm intensity. "Every time a hurricane comes in you have even more houses to blow down," says Easterling. Study the data rather than the hype and there's no sign yet that tropical storms are getting more frequent or more intense. Shock headlines notwithstanding, such storms are still rare, making the statistics hard to handle.

Rising Waters

Regardless of what global warming does to storms, sea level will definitely rise. It's already on the move, and some say that it will increase by as much as half a metre over the [twenty-first] century, thanks to expansion of the oceans and melting of land ice. "Storm surges test sea defences very severely," says Folland. "Even if storm levels stayed the same, increasing sea level will bring a much greater threat to low-lying areas around the world."

Putting more energy into the climate engine could also mean more rainfall, and hence more flooding. Mozambique was desperately unlucky when two tropical cyclones conspired to dump their water there [in 2000], while India was hit by a freakishly intense monsoon. Though global warming can't be fingered for any one disaster, there's already evidence that rainfall is becoming more widespread and more intense.

Tom Karl, also at the NCDC in North Carolina, published a paper in 1998 showing a marked increase, over the [twentieth] century in the number of days that saw heavy rainfall in the US. Easterling has seen a similar pattern for longer periods of rain. Overall, the US has seen increases in rain, hail and snow of up to 10 per cent.

This is in line with what the models predict. In 1997, Kevin Hennessy from the CSIRO [Commonwealth Scientific and Industrial Research Organisation] in Victoria, Australia, working with researchers from the Met Office in Britain, modelled the effect of warming on rainfall. He found that in high latitudes there should be more wet days every year, and that all rainstorms would become heavier. At middle and low latitudes there would be fewer wet days, but the rain that did fall would be more intense.

That could also bring more severe droughts. When you crank up the climate system everything becomes more extreme, and if rainstorms are more intense in one place, that could mean less rain somewhere else. So far, there is no sign in the records that droughts are increasing in frequency or severity. But the models predict that parts of the world—especially at low latitudes—will become steadily drier as the world warms.

Changing Weather Cycles

Even perfectly natural parts of the weather machine could be getting in on the global warming act. There are signs, for instance, that El Niño events are getting stronger. El Niños occur when a pool of warm water migrates across the Pacific, dumping torrential rain on the west coast of the Americas and leaving drought behind on the Asian side. The really strong El Niños cause havoc around the world. In 1998, for instance, Indonesia and the Amazon were ravaged by forest fires, Ecuador, Chile and Peru experienced intense rainfall, and Venezuela faced mudslides that were disastrous. Though the jury is still out on whether global warming could exacerbate El Niño events, they do seem to have become more frequent and more intense in the past few decades and some researchers believe warming is to blame.

Add all this together and the prospects for the future seem decidedly tempestuous. Should we batten down the hatches? "Prepare for change," says Folland. "We're not reducing our greenhouse gas emissions anything like fast enough to stop the effects of climate change this century. It's too late. We can slow warming down, but we can't stop it." All the signs are that change will mean more extreme weather. So if you think today's storms are wild, wait till global warming really kicks in. You ain't seen nothing yet.

THE POTENTIAL EFFECTS OF GLOBAL WARMING ON HUMAN HEALTH

Bruce Agnew

In the following selection Bruce Agnew explores how global warming may impact world health. According to the author, most scientists who have participated in recent climatological studies agree that global warming will affect the world's ecosystems and weather patterns. These climatic changes are likely to have detrimental effects on human health, he explains. For example, Agnew writes, global warming may cause droughts, floods, and other extreme weather conditions that can result in catastrophic loss of human life, interrupt food production, and contaminate water supplies. Furthermore, refugees fleeing from weather-damaged regions may move into already crowded locales, creating unsanitary conditions that foster the spread of infectious disease. In addition, he notes, poor nations—which have fewer resources to cope with health crises—are more likely to be affected by global warming than industrialized countries. Agnew is a science writer in Bethesda, Maryland.

Most climatologists now believe that the Earth's atmosphere is warming, but no one knows how high, or how fast, temperatures may rise. And even though several national and international studies [in 2001] predicted that tropical diseases such as malaria and dengue may extend their ranges as the world warms—and that disrupted storm and rainfall patterns may raise threats of everything from crop failures to cholera—no scientific consensus exists on precisely what ecological upsets will hit which countries, where, in the coming decades. Climate computer models cannot fine-tune their projections to regional levels that could tell local officials, for example, whether to prepare for droughts, or floods, or both.

But several major conclusions are clear. "What needs to be recognized is that there is very little doubt among leading scientists [who have taken part in recent studies] that climate change is a reality," says WHO [World Health Organization] environmental health expert

Bruce Agnew, "Planet Earth, Getting Too Hot for Health?" *Bulletin of the World Health Organization*, vol. 79, November 2001, p. 1,090. Copyright © 2001 by the World Health Organization. Reproduced by permission.

Dr Carlos Corvalan. "We don't yet know how severe the impacts are going to be or how accurate the predictions of environmental change are, but the evidence is accumulating, and ecological and human health impacts are expected. We are also concerned that the health impacts of global warming will strike hardest at developing nations, particularly the poorest."

A nation's ability to adapt to climate change "depends on such factors as wealth, technology, education, information, skills, infrastructure, access to resources, and management capabilities," says the Third Assessment Report of the United Nations Intergovernmental Panel on Climate Change (IPCC), released early [in 2001]. "The developing countries, particularly the least developed countries, are generally poorest in this regard."

A Complex Task

It is also clear that preparing for global warming is going to be an immensely complex task. Global warming "will require attention on many fronts," says Dr Jonathan Patz, director of the programme on health effects of global environmental change at the Johns Hopkins Bloomberg School of Public Health in Baltimore, Maryland, USA.

In particular, global warming will place huge new demands on public health officials and governmental health ministries, says Dr Bettina Menne, global change officer of the WHO European Centre for Environment and Health in Rome. Up until now, she says, most studies of the multiple, interlocking risk factors posed by warming have been driven "not by the public health people but by [computer] modellers, mathematicians and climatologists or economists." The public health community must become more deeply involved in these assessments, she says.

At least, the modellers, mathematicians and climatologists have filled in the background. The IPCC's report projected that unless world governments take steps to stabilize emissions of carbon dioxide and other greenhouse gases, the global average surface temperature will rise by 1.4 degrees C to 5.8 degrees C (2.5 degrees F to 10.8 degrees F) between 1990 and 2100—a pace of warming that the report said is "very likely" unprecedented over the past 10,000 years.

Scientific Consensus

The IPCC's Working Group I, which involved nearly 1000 scientists, predicted these changes: land areas will warm more rapidly than the oceans, particularly at high latitudes; precipitation will increase globally, with heavy precipitation over most land areas; in some areas precipitation will decline; and the sea level will rise by 9–88 centimetres between 1990 and 2100. "Extreme weather events"—such as heatwaves, heavy rains, floods, droughts, more ferocious hurricanes and typhoons, and drying out of soil at mid-latitudes—will likely increase, but current climate models cannot tell precisely where they will strike, the IPCC report said.

These projections are based on computer models that still have some gaps and uncertainties, but the scientific consensus supporting the forecast of a warmer world has become overwhelming. Even in the US, where global warming at times has been a political issue, the influential National Academy of Sciences signed on to the IPCC warming projections in June [2001]. After a review requested by US President George Bush, a National Academy of Sciences committee reported: "The body of the [IPCC Working Group I] report is scientifically credible and is not unlike what would be produced by a comparable group of only US scientists working with a similar set of emission scenarios, with perhaps some normal differences in scientific tone and emphasis."

Assessing what global warming will mean for human health, however, is a hugely complex task, clouded by uncertainties. "One of the difficulties," says Patz, "is that we are talking about complex modes of exposure to the risk factors, and we're talking about long-term risk factors."

"If you raise the temperature a few degrees," Patz explains, "not only will that have an immediate physical effect on humans—especially on the elderly in urban areas—but raising the temperature changes atmospheric chemistry, which then can affect air pollution, especially tropospheric [low-level] ozone. Changes in temperature and precipitation can affect ecology and habitat for insect vectors of diseases. Warmer air holds more moisture, causing more extremes in the water cycle, giving you both droughts and flooding, affecting runoff and contamination, for example, from agriculture."

The Health Effects of Global Warming

Nevertheless, a series of international and national studies—and not a few individual scientists—have tried to puzzle out global warming's likely health effects. In addition to the IPCC effort, these include a WHO study [in 2000] titled "Climate change and human health: impact and adaptation", as well as government-sponsored national assessments in the UK, the US and several other countries. The US National Academy of Sciences, too, conducted a separate study on global warming and infectious diseases that was published in April [2001]. Among the climate-triggered health threats that the studies spotlight are these:

• Vector-borne infectious diseases—such as malaria, dengue, schistosomiasis, leishmaniasis and encephalitis—may alter their geographical ranges and seasonality, spreading into new regions and declining in others. But some vector-borne disease experts say too many factors are involved in insect and disease organism life cycles to make projections based primarily on climatic changes.

• Heat-related deaths could rise in response to more frequent and more intense heat-waves, particularly in temperate-zone cities and among the elderly and urban poor who lack adequate air conditioning. But little research has been conducted on heat stress in developing countries, and scientists are only now beginning to examine heat morbidity—illness and disability short of death.

• Cold-related mortality might decline. In at least some temperate-zone countries, this reduction in cold-weather deaths might offset the increase in heat-stress mortality. But Johns Hopkins' Patz suspects that the lives saved wouldn't balance lives lost.

• Air pollution in urban areas would likely rise as air temperatures warm—particularly the concentration of ground-level ozone, which is damaging to respiratory health and is a main component of urban smog. At the same time, if current scientific understanding is correct, warming of the atmosphere at low levels would actually cool the stratosphere, accelerating the destruction of the stratospheric ozone that protects the planet from damaging ultraviolet radiation. Shifts in local weather also could alter regional pollution patterns and the spread of airborne allergens such as pollens and mould spores.

• Extreme weather events could "play a more significant role than even the warming itself in creating conditions conducive to outbreaks of disease," says Dr Paul Epstein, associate director of the Center for Health and the Public Environment at the Harvard Medical School in Boston, Massachusetts, USA. In addition to direct injury, and loss of life, violent weather can destroy shelter, contaminate water supplies, cripple food production, foster myriad infectious diseases, and tear apart existing health service infrastructures.

• Population displacement, forced by rising sea levels or extreme weather or agricultural collapse, would complicate the public health challenge. Large numbers of refugees moving into already populated areas, crowded together, hungry and perhaps starving, without shelter or adequate sanitation, is a formula for spreading infectious disease and promoting social conflict. "Personally I think that population displacement will be the iceberg under the tip of this problem," says Patz. "The displaced population issue could be the toughest and largest public health issue of climate change, yet it is without doubt the most difficult to put our arms around."

• Malnutrition risks, and the diseases that accompany malnutrition, would rise as agricultural practices adapt to new patterns of temperature, rainfall and soil-moisture conditions. Improved farm production in some regions, including northern Europe, might balance losses elsewhere. "But the risk of reduced food yields is greatest in developing countries—where 790 million people are estimated to be undernourished at present," the IPCC report says.

• Warming oceans could promote more frequent toxic algal blooms, increase the incidence of diarrhoeal diseases, and spread the risk of poisonings from fish and shellfish toxins that now are mostly limited to tropical waters.

• Emerging infectious diseases—not just known diseases such as Ebola haemorrhagic fever but also new diseases that science has not yet recognized—might be set free by ecosystem changes in response to shifting local weather conditions, providing new niches for non-native micro-organisms. Ecological systems that are upset might also spur the evolution of new strains of disease organisms, according to the US National Academy of Sciences study of linkages between climate, ecosystems and infectious disease in the United States.

"More people are expected to be harmed than benefited by climate change, even for global mean temperature increases of less than a few degrees," says the IPCC report. (And citizens of the poorer nations worst of all. Patz bristles at "the incredible inequity of this problem. The developed countries that are burning the most fossil fuel are the root of the problem, and yet it's the small island nations, the developing countries, that are really going to bear its brunt.")

Solving the Problem

So what's to be done?

At this early stage in science's understanding of global warming and its effects, no one seems to have a good answer to that question. Or at least, no one knows enough, yet, about the specific health problems that global warming may bring, to propose any detailed answers now. But there are a lot of wish-lists.

More research is first on every list: meteorological studies and development of better computer models to narrow down the specific, regional weather effects of climate change; improved surveillance of diseases like malaria and dengue, both to create a good database on their extent and to provide early warning of any spread of their ranges; new studies of the transmission dynamics of vector-, rodent- and waterborne diseases; and "integrative research" that takes into account the complex interactions within (and between) physical, ecological and societal systems that may make them vulnerable to climate change. The list of potential research subjects goes on and on.

"There's a lot of research that needs to be done, and some practical problems to study," says Harvard's Epstein. For example, "given what we already know about floods and mosquito-borne diseases, floods and cholera and waterborne diseases, there's a lot that we should be doing some real field work on."

It's also important now "to consider not just the potential impacts but to begin addressing adaptation measures", says WHO's Corvalan. "There's a realization that countries will need to take measures, as early as possible, to adapt to the potential changes, including changes to the health sector and delivery of health services. We need 'no-regrets' solutions, where benefits are achieved regardless of the magnitude of predicted impacts." This was the objective of a . . . WHO workshop on small island countries organized in Samoa by Corvalan, Patz and Dr Hisashi Ogawa from WHO's Western Pacific regional office.

In addition, WHO's European regional office is conducting a three-year, 25-nation study of whether the preventive mechanisms are in place to cope with climate change. But Menne says the question of adaptation must be raised globally.

Adaptation will be costly. That's why developing nations are expected to have a harder time than the richer industrialized nations that can afford, and that already have, elaborate public health infrastructures.

But there may be a silver lining.

"Most of the actions that are needed to adapt to the impacts of climate change—such as stepped-up vector-control efforts, improved water treatment systems and enhanced disaster-relief capability—would improve our health," says Dr Pim Martens, director of the Global Assessment Centre of Maastricht University's International Centre for Integrative Studies in the Netherlands, "even without global warming."

GLOBAL WARMING IN THE ANTARCTIC

Charles W. Petit

Charles W. Petit writes for *U.S. News & World Report*. For the following article, he traveled to Palmer Station, an American research facility located on the Antarctic Peninsula, to investigate the impact of global warming. Petit reports that while the Antarctic is still one of the coldest places in the world, it is warming more rapidly than the rest of the planet. Moreover, he states, this warming trend has already produced dramatic effects: Icebergs are shrinking, glaciers are receding, and the immense Larsen Ice Shelf is quickly collapsing into the ocean. Researchers have also discovered alarming fluctuations in wildlife populations that they believe are due to global warming. For example, Petit relates, the local population of Adelie penguins appears to be dying off because the birds have been unable to adjust to environmental changes in their habitat. According to the author, although scientists are still unsure what the long-term effects of the changing conditions in the Antarctic will be, they have little doubt that global warming is responsible.

One doesn't need a Ph.D. to see that things are changing fast around here. "That's Dead Seal Point up there," says Ross Hein, 27, director of boating operations at this remote American research base. On a sunny January day—midsummer in Antarctica—he points the Zodiac inflated motorboat toward a low, rocky islet a mile or so east of the base. The tough, flexible bow bumps slowly through a shoal of ice chunks—some the size of golf balls, others as big as a refrigerator—shoved near shore by the wind and current. The hard ice gives the boat a ride like an old truck on a bad road. It leads into a startlingly beautiful passage several hundred yards long and 50 yards wide. "Two years ago," Hein marvels, "this wasn't even here."

The point is that Dead Seal Point has no point, for we clearly are passing behind an island. To the right is a long wall of extravagantly fractured ice high as a 10-story building. It is the leading edge of Marr

Ice Piedmont, a glacial cap that reaches a depth of 2,000 feet on 38-mile-long Anvers Island, Palmer's home 120 miles outside the Antarctic Circle. Hein, to minimize hazards from falling ice, keeps well to the left, along a miniature, melting ice cap atop Dead Seal Point.

The spot's name stems, first, from the now vanished elephant seal that died on its seaward side a few years ago. But what is more significant, the rock was once believed to be a peninsular point peeking from under the glacier's foot. Since the 1960s, Anvers Island's glacial mantle has pulled its skirts in by about 30 feet annually. The point turned out to be an island, one of many emerging along the shore. Thirty years ago, the then new Palmer Station was about 50 yards from the same retreating glacial front. Now it is a quarter-mile walk. An eerily beautiful ice cave nearby, today about 40 yards long and formed by a drainage channel along the glacier's base, was twice as long a decade ago.

Antarctic Heat Wave

If you think a few degrees of global warming would not mean much in your neighborhood, the word from Palmer Station is: Think again. While hardly warm here, what with icebergs like ivory cathedrals turning majestically in adjacent Arthur Harbor, it may be the most warmed-up place on the planet. It provides lessons for us all if, as many scientists believe, Earth is unstoppably entering a heat wave that could last centuries.

The Antarctic Peninsula is an S-shaped projection of mountains, geologically related to the Andes, that reaches 800 miles north from the main continent toward South America. The computerized climate models used to forecast global warming reveal no reason for this place to be warming more rapidly than the rest of the planet. But since the mid-1940s, the average year-round temperature on the peninsula has gone up 3 to 4 degrees Fahrenheit, and in the early winter (June in the Southern Hemisphere) it is up a startling 7 to 9 degrees. While it still snows year-round, with summer temperatures averaging a few degrees above freezing and the middle of winter running in the teens, the rate of warming is 10 times the global average.

The bulk of the continent has only warmed a degree or so in the same time. Even this is enough to make some climate scientists worry that a significant part of its ice cap could someday melt, raising sea levels precariously. But there is no sign of that yet, and the South Pole itself, atop a 2-mile-thick layer of ice where temperatures stay well below zero, may actually have cooled a bit. Such inconsistency is among reasons skeptics assert that global warming is too uncertain to merit costly programs to contain it.

But here warming is no mere hypothesis. And one senses how high the stakes are if the skeptics are wrong. The local warm-up is already in the same ballpark as that which the Intergovernmental Panel on Climate Change—set up in 1988 by the United Nations and the World

Meteorological Organization to advise politicians—expects for the rest of the world during the next century.

Obvious Changes

The changes aren't subtle. One hundred miles to the east, on the other side of the Antarctic Peninsula, the immense and supposedly permanent Larsen Ice Shelf began to disintegrate in 1995. Nearly 1,000 square miles of shelf have collapsed just in the past two years, with thousands of square miles more appearing ready to go. "Climate change showed up on the radar screen 30 years ago or so, but most people back then never thought we'd really have to worry about it," says Bill Fraser, a tall, rangy ecologist and penguin specialist from Montana State University. He is the station's chief scientist and has been coming down here for two decades. "Now, right here, we're basically confirming what the models back then said would happen if climate changed. The species most vulnerable, those at the edges of their natural ranges, would be affected first. And that is what is happening."

In recent years, hints of wildlife migrations and local extinctions have been picked up around the world—butterflies moving to new ranges, for instance, or plants moving to higher altitudes on mountains. But the picture here is simpler and starker. Not only is warming greater but, except for the occasional scientist or carefully monitored tourist, direct human impact is scant. So one cannot blame wildlife changes on factors like toxic pollution, agriculture, or urbanization.

And wildlife shifts are unmistakable. Around Palmer and elsewhere on the western side of the peninsula there is not only less ice but a new set of residents. Southern elephant seals—the males are massive, sluglike beasts that can reach 8,800 pounds—usually raise their young farther north in more temperate climes like the Falkland Islands. But one day [in the summer of 1999], 254 elephant seals, including many pups, were seen on just two islands near Palmer, with uncounted others presumably living up and down the coast. More hospitable weather is the only explanation scientists have for this sudden migration southward.

Fur seals, too, were not reported here before midcentury. But [in 1995], a research vessel counted 2,000 of them on just one island farther south. Similarly, gentoo penguins and chinstrap penguins, species common closer to South America but virtually absent in fossil deposits around Palmer, are establishing new colonies on the peninsula. And while nobody expects forests to appear on these icy plains, low grass, tiny shrubs, and mosses are thickening rapidly in many areas of the peninsula.

To see what such rapid heating does to a landscape and its wildlife, a *U.S. News & World Report* team visited Palmer in January [2000], the height of austral summer. The peninsula has no airstrip, so it takes four days from Punta Arenas, Chile, across the Drake Passage aboard the

Laurence M. Gould, an oceanographic research and resupply vessel under charter to the National Science Foundation. NSF manages the $200 million-per-year U.S. Antarctic program, and Palmer is one of the agency's premier sites for studying long-term ecological change.

Research in the Antarctic

At a glance the region looks much as it did to American seal hunter Nathaniel Palmer and other explorers who saw this part of the world in the 1820s. Palmer Station's small cluster of blue, corrugated steel buildings perch upon a rocky shore. Behind them the glacier extends as far as the eye can see. Inside the friendly base are laboratories, warm bunks, a good kitchen, and the "Penguin Pub" bar. Over the pool table is an old whale's rib, and above the fridge is an orange life preserver from the Argentine ship *Bahia Paraiso*, which sank after hitting nearby rocks in 1989. Its hulk is still visible from the station at low tide, and it still smells of the oil that wiped out a cormorant colony in the weeks after the wreck. Outside, gale-force winds can pour down the glacier without warning, sucking the warmth from anybody caught outside and not bundled up.

Palmer, with a maximum population of around 40 and an annual cost of $12 million, is one of three U.S. Antarctic stations and the only one on the peninsula. The main U.S. headquarters is McMurdo Station, nearly 2,500 miles away on the Ross Sea, where the population can exceed 1,000 people, and the other station is at the South Pole. Like all of Antarctica, the peninsula is a utopia of international cooperation. No one needs a passport to be here. The 1959 Antarctic Treaty suspended all territorial claims and reserved the great white continent for scientific research.

Fraser, 49, came here as a grad student and soon after did a 14-month sojourn. He makes no secret of the fact that he loves Adelie penguins. Changes here are not limited to new species moving in. Indeed, the Adelies are dying off, and fast.

Imagine a flock of turkeys trying to bleat like sheep, amplify it a few times, and that is the sound of a colony of Adelies. They are packed into nests of small pebbles stained pink with guano, and one often smells their raucous colonies before hearing them. Analysis of debris under nesting sites indicates that Adelies have dominated bird life around here for at least 600 years. And, to a first-time visitor during nesting season, Adelies seem to be waddling comically everywhere on the small offshore islands or slicing swiftly through the waves and dodging fierce leopard seals that prey upon them.

But 25 years ago more than 15,000 pairs of the penguins nested yearly within about 2 miles of the base. This year, there are about 7,700 of the handsome, formal-clad couples raising young. The population is down 10 percent in just the past two years. One soon learns to recognize the silent expanses of pebbles that mark extinct colonies.

Penguin Diets

On Torgersen Island, about half a mile west of Palmer, Fraser quietly watches and counts the birds as they come and go or tend their nests and their chicks. The chicks are about two-thirds the size of an adult and covered in gray down. But in addition to taking a census of the Adelies, Fraser wants to know what the birds are eating. "You know how the old-timers did this?" he asks. He takes aim down an imaginary rifle barrel. "Plink! I just don't think I could ever do that. No way."

Instead, he and co-researcher Donna Patterson select five of the 18-inch-high Adelies as they hop across the rocks, tummies plump from foraging at sea. After a short chase, they drop a net over each bird, pick it up by the base of a flipper, and carefully measure its skull and beak size. While Fraser grips the bird's torso between his knees, Patterson gets behind him to hold its calloused, sharp-nailed feet. Field assistant and graduate student Erik Chapman dips a clear, flexible tube in olive oil. He passes the tube to Fraser, who with a look of apology on his face, slides it down the penguin's throat. Turning a hand crank, Chapman pumps warm salt water into the bird's stomach. In a moment, the bird regurgitates the water, along with its recent meal.

Bird by bird, the researchers fill small plastic bags with disgorged krill, the shrimplike plankton that are the near-exclusive fare of penguins here. Except for a slight pink color from exposure to digestive enzymes and acids, the limp crustaceans look fresh. A pair of brown skuas—powerful predatory relatives of gulls that fly like eagles and often consume stray penguin chicks—alight nearby. They know they'll get some leftovers tossed to the ground by the scientists. As far as can be told, the procedure does the penguins no harm. They endure it with impressive equanimity. Upon release, each scrambles away, flippers flapping, then resumes a deliberate walk back to the colony where mate and offspring wait.

An hour or so later, Bill, Donna, and Erik are back at a lab bench on Palmer's ground floor, picking through the erstwhile penguin meals with tweezers, measuring each of the krill against a ruler. To the untrained eye they don't look ominous—fat and near the 2.5-inch maximum length that these krill reach. But Fraser sees something else. "This looks bad," he says, laying a few krill upon the lab bench's black surface. Such big krill are at least three years old. Young krill depend in their first winter on shelter under the solid ice that forms on the sea surface. The absence of young krill in these Adelies' diet reinforces Fraser's fear that this food source could collapse if winters around here remain as warm and ice free as they have become. Recently, winter ice is getting rarer. At midcentury 4 out of every 5 winters here produced extensive sea ice. Now, just 2 in 5 bring the heavy winter ice necessary to shelter the young krill.

As early as the mid-'80s, researchers at Palmer could see the local Adelie population dropping. At the same time, chinstrap penguins, almost unknown here before the late 1950s, were (and are) prospering, sometimes walking right into Adelie rookeries and setting up housekeeping flipper to flipper with their cousin species. And while krill may be down, both penguins eat them, so a food shortage seemed an unlikely way to explain their differing fates. Except for a dark line under their beaks, chinstraps look a lot like Adelies. And for a long time scientists knew of no significant behavioral differences between the species that would explain why one might do better than the other. A big clue came in the coldest, darkest months of 1988. That year the U.S.-chartered research vessel Polar Duke explored the Weddell Sea on the east side of the Antarctic Peninsula. The expedition, with Fraser on board, found the winter ice pack swarming with Adelie penguins. By contrast, the open sea glittered with chinstraps. Until then nobody knew that Adelies depend on sea ice to get through the winter, feeding on krill around its edges. In recent years, as sea ice has become scarcer around Palmer, it became apparent why the region's Adelies were struggling while the chinstraps flourished.

But that's not the Adelies' only problem. By nature, Adelies are hard-wired for a narrow and inflexible range of behavior, as an anecdote from several winters ago illustrates. The icebreaker encountered perhaps 2,000 Adelies marching along single file. As the ship pulled even with the marchers, the lead bird reached a gap in the ice perhaps a foot across. It hesitated, hopped over, tripped on a small bump, fell flat on its face, popped up, and kept going. "Damned if every single penguin didn't jump at exactly the same place and do a face plant exactly like the first one," Fraser recalls. "Bam, bam, bam." Not one Adelie thought to cross just 5 inches to the left or right. "That says something about the intelligence of Adelies," Fraser said.

This is more than a humorous story to Fraser. It demonstrates that, even more than many other penguins, this species has evolved very inflexible habits. "That is a boon in a fragile and tough environment where, once one finds a good niche, it pays off to stick with it," Fraser explains. "But it is a behavioral flaw in times of climate change."

Creatures of Habit

Around Palmer, he sees evidence on every visit to the rookeries of the Adelies' inability to adjust to surprises. The birds live a dozen years or longer and mate for life. Once a pair establishes a nesting site—most commonly on the same island where they were born and often in the same colony—the couple usually returns to the exact same nesting place year after year.

But warmer air holds more moisture, and in this still-cold place, that means more snow. Prevailing winds here pile snow deepest on the southwest-facing sides of the small islands where the penguins nest. The birds there seem incapable of recognizing, in the deepening snow, that it is time to set up housekeeping somewhere else. When spring arrives in September and October, the Adelies often—and stubbornly—pile pebbles atop snow 2 feet thick or more to build their nests. Later, frigid meltwater kills eggs and newborn chicks by the score. By contrast, chinstraps seem a bit more flexible in where they nest, choosing sites based more on their immediate suitability.

During a penguin-counting survey on Cormorant Island, Patterson points to a tiny remnant Adelie outpost. It has two nests, surrounded by a penumbra of smoothed pebbles where hundreds of penguins raised their young 10 years ago. And standing about insolently are half a dozen brown skuas, waiting for a chance to grab a lightly defended baby penguin. Maps of Adelie colonies consistently show that most of the failed colonies are located where snows have become deepest. The chicks born in these places are hatched later and are smaller. Chicks from colonies on northern-facing shores weigh an average of nearly 7 pounds; those on snowier south shores are a pound lighter. "Lightweight chicks won't survive their first winter," Fraser says.

Every failed penguin colony could be just one more local chapter in the pitiless pageant of nature. Certainly, there are no endangered species here. Adelies are flourishing at the southern end of their range in the Ross Sea. And that fits the climate-change model, too. The Ross Sea historically has been so bitterly cold that a little warming there makes it more, not less, hospitable to the Adelies. "Their whole range," Fraser observes, "seems to be shifting south."

But in most of the world, the natural ranges of species cannot move as easily as they can in this vast, unspoiled continent. If warmer weather drives a species to the edge of a city, or to the top of a mountain, that may be the end of it. And that's why the lessons from the Adelies here should demand attention elsewhere.

Palmer is one of several sites in the Long-Term Ecological Research program, sponsored by NSF to keep track of how wildlife in specific areas is doing. While Fraser has been there longest, other Palmer-based scientists track the richness of the bottom of the food chain, including marine algae and other plankton in the sea, the krill that feed on plankton, and microbes living in the water, ice, and thin soil.

The Ozone Effect

Temperature and snowfall are not the only changing environmental factors here, either. The famed ozone hole, a loss of ultraviolet-absorbing ozone molecules in the stratosphere over Antarctica, affects the Palmer area in October and November each year. Ultraviolet radiation levels soar. University of Texas graduate student Jarah Meador found so many bacteria living in the glacier fragments floating in the harbor that she e-mailed Wade Jeffrey of the University of West Florida, principal investigator on a program to monitor the effects of ultraviolet radiation on Antarctic microbes. He had a plan.

One sunny day, after some training in rappelling down ice cliffs with the base search-and-rescue team, Meador hiked up the glacier behind the base and lowered herself on a rope down a narrow crevasse that extended 100 feet into the ice. "It's great down there," she exulted on the way back out. In the deep blue light filtering through the ice, she dug into the vertical wall of ice at intervals, carefully preventing contamination while she gathered samples. If the microbes at great depth turn out to be different from those near the surface, it could mean that evolution is already retuning the microbes to tolerate increased levels of ultraviolet radiation.

No one yet knows how or whether the ozone hole is a major threat to the region's biology. But there is little doubt about warming and penguins. After a few decades watching the same population of birds—he is now studying great grandchicks of some of his first ones—Fraser says he is beginning to feel, in his bones, what he calls ecological time: the decades to centuries over which populations ebb, flow, and sometimes vanish. At one of the station's evening science seminars, physicist Dan Lubin of Scripps Institution of Oceanography, at Palmer to study how ice and open sea reflect sunlight, notes that climate change does not appear or disappear quickly. The atmosphere's carbon dioxide and other solar-energy-trapping gases won't return to preindustrial levels for 200 years or more, even if humans could somehow stop their emissions right now. "Two hundred years!" Fraser says. "Even in ecological time, that is enough to really screw things up."

THE IMPACT OF GLOBAL WARMING ON ARCTIC COMMUNITIES

Gordon Laird

In the following selection, Canadian writer and photojournalist Gordon Laird examines the effects of rising global temperatures on Arctic communities. Laird reports that the cold season is beginning later and ending sooner in the Arctic, which has created problems as minor as delaying the ice hockey season and as profound as homelessness. He explains that global warming is especially threatening to the Inuit, the native people of the Arctic region. Many Inuit still rely on hunting for survival, but warmer-than-usual temperatures have drastically shortened the winter hunting season and adversely affected wildlife habitats. As seal and other game have grown scarce, a number of hunters have become impoverished or even homeless, the author states. Global warming threatens to destroy the cultural heritage and traditions of the people of the Artic, he concludes. Laird is the author of the book *Power: Journeys Across an Energy Nation*.

As a snow squall blows in from Greenland, a crowd huddles inside the Iqaluit Municipal Arena while the skaters wait for the puck to drop. It's the start of the annual [Baffin] Island hockey tournament and Iqaluit, the capital of Canada's self-governed Inuit province, Nunavut, faces off against Pond Inlet, a remote settlement 800 miles to the north. Skates flashing, teenage boys scramble up and down the ice, hoping to prove themselves in front of the capital city fans.

Hockey is the premier team sport in Nunavut, a place where both dogsleds and desktop computers are common household items. Communities that once met on the pack ice during hunting forays now await the passing of the Zamboni together, bundled up in fur-fringed parkas and kamiks. Iqaluit boasts one of the province's two artificial ice surfaces; everyone else plays the old-fashioned way, on outdoor rinks that usually freeze solid by the time the season begins in November.

But the last several winters have brought a crisis for Nunavut hockey. Temperatures across the territory have hovered near or above

Gordon Laird, "Losing the Cool," *Mother Jones*, vol. 27, March/April 2002, pp. 76–79. Copyright © 2002 by the Foundation for National Progress. Reproduced by permission.

freezing long into the Arctic winter, keeping many teams benched until Christmas. [In 2000], the provincial hockey association called for help from Canada's hockey authorities because 50 percent of its members had yet to start playing and paying their dues. Even villages well north of the Arctic Circle couldn't cobble together enough ice time to field a team. And with temperatures once again reaching record highs across the continent's northern regions, the winter [of 2002] has proved to be another troublesome season.

Accelerated Warming

The slushy ice and erratic weather that have been frustrating Nunavut's hockey players are part of a larger set of climatic trends that are playing out throughout the Arctic. Sea ice—the frozen ocean surface that human and animal hunters traverse in search of their prey—is more mobile and fragile than it was a decade ago. Disoriented polar bears wander inland at times when they would normally be prowling the floes for seal. Skies are cloudier, rain falls more often, and locals report the arrival of species never seen before, such as robins.

Only a few weeks before my visit to Nunavut early [in 2001], the U.N. Intergovernmental Panel on Climate Change [IPCC] unveiled its latest evaluation of climate science around the world. The panel's report echoed and amplified the commission's previous warnings: The global warming trend measured throughout the 1990s had accelerated far past earlier estimates. On average, the scientists predicted, the planet could see a rise in average temperatures of 11 degrees by 2100, an increase "without precedent during the last 10,000 years." An even more dramatic warm-up, two to three times as fast, was forecast for Greenland, Alaska, and Arctic Canada.

The warming has already begun. Over the past 30 years, winter temperatures in parts of the north have risen more than 10 degrees, compared to a worldwide increase of just 1 degree. The volume of ice in the polar cap has decreased 40 percent since American submarines first took measurements in 1958. Some researchers predict that if greenhouse-gas emissions continue unabated, summer ice over the North Pole could disappear by 2050—a catastrophic melt that, under one long-term scenario, could raise oceans by up to 21 feet worldwide.

The U.N. panel's findings barely made the news in the United States, where the Bush administration was preparing to withdraw from worldwide climate-change negotiations. But in Nunavut, the report confirmed what hunters, hockey players, and traditional elders already knew all too well. For the people of the Arctic have been the first among us to learn what it means to live in a greenhouse world.

Threatening the Way of Life

As Pond Inlet sets up to play Cape Dorset, I wander out into Iqaluit's late-winter twilight. It's minus 35, and global warming feels like a distant rumor. Caribou-skinclad hunters roar down the streets on snow-mobiles while taxis and pickup trucks line up at the town's main inter-section. Polar-bear hides are stretched outside near a Pizza Hut outlet.

Around the corner from the hockey arena is the one-room hut of Iqaluit's Hunters and Trappers Association. In a space crowded with caribou tags, a Coleman stove, and a computer, association manager David Audlakiak is busy tracking this season's polar-bear kills. Only nine kills have been logged since the season opened. It's been a slow start, mostly because nearby Frobisher Bay froze six weeks late.

"Weather for hunters has a lot to do with how much they can har-vest," explains Audlakiak. "For my family, it takes longer to get fresh seal in the bay. We cannot have seal unless the ice can support our weight." In the past, hunters could trust the ice by late October, but this season they did not go out until December—a delay that cost many families a key part of their winter income.

The changes come at a bad time for communities where hunting is a matter of survival. Only 40 years ago, many Arctic towns relied on seal and other animals for most of their basic needs. But a housing crunch, rising food and gas prices, and a slumping fur market have forced a growing number of hunters to turn to Canada's form of wel-fare. Problems familiar to other native communities, like alcoholism and diabetes, are all on the rise in Nunavut. "The hunter just here was homeless," Audlakiak confides during a lull in the stream of visitors to his office. "Our families have limited supplies to share, only hot cof-fee and bannock sometimes. We feel like we are unwanted children."

Now, elders warn, climate change and other environmental prob-lems pose the most serious threat yet to Inuit tradition. "This is a mat-ter of health and cultural heritage," says Sheila Watt-Cloutier, president of Canada's Inuit Circumpolar Conference. "It's not just about store-bought food. It's about losing the hunting and the connection to the land—and the incredible learning and teaching that the land offers."

When we spoke [in] spring [2001], Watt-Cloutier had just returned from South Africa, where she had helped engineer the Stockholm Convention—an international agreement to eliminate emissions of dioxins, PCBs, and 10 other toxic compounds that have been drifting to the Arctic from the industrial regions of Europe and North Amer-ica. "The climate-change issue will be a lot more challenging for us," Watt-Cloutier admitted, "because it's bigtime industry. How much will they be willing to give up in terms of money and control?"

Changes in the Ice

The high Arctic settlement of Resolute Bay speeds past as Hans Aron-sen sleds me out onto the ice of the Northwest Passage. It's minus 45, with a wind chill of minus 91, and Aronsen, a local polar-bear guide, guns the snowmobile into the gale. At 2 P.M. the sun has already dis-appeared, leaving a glorious trail of pink, orange, and red.

I've flown 1,000 miles north from Iqaluit to this town on Cornwallis Island, where 180 people support themselves by hunting and catering to adventure travelers. This is the gateway to Canada's high Arctic islands, a largely uninhabited land of glaciers and mountains, musk oxen and polar bears.

Out on the ice, Aronsen surveys the scene. The sheltered bay is a smooth, snow-covered plain; beyond it lies a jumbled maze of rough first-year ice. In the past, large parts of the passage never thawed, and the multi-year ice provided a surface free of shelves, fissures, and pile-ups. Now, it is an obstacle course that only polar bears seem to appreciate. "Bears use the bad ice to hunt, but we get caught up in it," Aronsen explains. What's more, spring thaws have come early in recent years, leaving hunters too little time to work the wildlife-rich floes. "For the last three seasons when the ice breaks, it disappears and stays gone," he says.

According to Canada's environmental agency, Resolute Bay has seen a series of mini–heat waves in the last several years, with temperatures as much as 32 degrees above normal. In 1998, the warmest year on record worldwide, stretches of pack ice 10 feet thick disappeared in a single season. "Ice that has remained in place for the last 20 years melted and was flushed out," reports Thomas Agnew, a climatologist at the agency. "This was some of the oldest in the Arctic basin."

A few days before my trek with Aronsen, Wayne Davidson, the government weather officer for Resolute Bay, showed me satellite pictures documenting a series of "rolling fissures," large waves of fractured ice, breaking along the Arctic Ocean. The phenomenon, known to the Inuit as pitunirk, has been around for eons, but the frozen waves are getting more frequent. "The warmer it is, the crazier the ice goes," Davidson says. "A few explorers got caught in this in 1999. They said it was like a continual explosion—huge, booming waves of energy. The whole thing is moving."

Aronsen stops the sled next to a circle of stakes and leather harnesses scattered about the ice. Piles of fur are curled up beneath the snow; as we approach, the dogs awaken and begin to howl. It's not just to impress American big-game hunters that Aronsen has recently returned to using an old-fashioned dogsled. "A komatik is safer on thinning ice," he says.

Unfamiliar Territory

Back in town his wife, Zipporah Kalluk Aronsen, explains that the shifting weather has scrambled traditional navigation and weather-forecasting systems. Like most Inuit, her family paid close attention to ice, clouds, and temperature. Every hunter was a meteorologist. "Today many can't understand what's happening," she says. "They could once tell the weather, but not anymore."

The uncertainty has elders concerned. "I feel that the earth has shifted," says Kalluk Aronsen's brother, David Ooingoot Kalluk, who has hunted the Northwest Passage for more than 40 years. As Ooingoot Kalluk recounts the changes of the past decade, his Inuktitut translated by his daughter Tracy, it becomes clear that his native landscape isn't just getting warmer—it's becoming strange, unfamiliar territory. "It's brighter now than it was before," he says. "And during the summer for the past six years, there are no low or high tides for three days. The water wasn't doing anything. Currents are frozen."

At the weather station, Davidson says meteorologists can confirm, but not explain, the reports of experienced hunters like Ooingoot Kalluk. By his own observation, winter days are lasting about 45 minutes longer than computer projections indicate they should; recent increases in temperature, he speculates, may cause changes in light refraction in the atmosphere. Other phenomena such as stronger pitunirk and shifting currents might be caused by the massive amounts of broken ice that have been flushing south each summer, piling up hundreds of feet thick and wreaking havoc with tides. Each year since 1998, the Canadian Ice Service has watched the breakup creep further north; by 2001 the melting reached all the way to Nansen Sound, Canada's most northerly ocean passage.

Recording Climate Change

Several days later, I travel another 400 miles north into the 24-hour darkness of Ellesmere Island, where a posse of scientists sits atop a mountain and studies the stratosphere for clues to ozone depletion and climate change. Here at Environment Canada's Eureka weather station, instruments have recorded many of the climate-change symptoms listed in the U.N. reports—rising temperatures, stronger winds, more moisture in the air.

For the researchers who make their home on this patch of ice and rock, those data are more than markings on a chart. Their high-tech Astrolab was built to take advantage of reliably clear skies in a "polar desert" that receives less precipitation than parts of the Sahara. But in recent years, cloud cover and snowstorms have increasingly interfered with observation. And in the summer, staffers are warned about mud slides: Unprecedented permafrost melts have caused 30-foot blocks of frozen earth to liquefy over the course of a few seasons.

A growing number of scientists see the Arctic as a kind of global thermostat, the source of much of the Northern Hemisphere's weather—and many worry that the region's rapid warming could flip a climatic switch, to disastrous effect. "The consequences of such a change defy prediction," Columbia University climate scientist Wallace Broecker has noted. "By adding greenhouse gases to the atmosphere, we are poking an angry beast."

Already, the Astrolab's instruments have detected some signs of a meteorological chain reaction. One of the lab's principal objects of study is the polar vortex, a permanent cyclone approximately the size of Africa that hovers 20 to 30 miles above the polar cap. The vortex has grown stronger in recent years, and so have the polar winds it spins off; those winds, in turn, pick up moisture from the thawing Arctic Ocean and transport it southward. This is how many Europeans and North Americans experience "global warming."

Complicated weather systems like the polar vortex make it hard to say how climate change will continue to play out, in the Arctic or elsewhere—a conundrum that frustrates researchers like Astrolab manager Vivek Voora. "So climate change isn't 100 percent certain," he says. "Why isn't 90 or 95 percent good enough? It's like the tobacco issue: We've debated it for ages. We just need to do something about it."

For some of the Arctic's longtime inhabitants, it may already be too late. Back in Resolute Bay, David Ooingoot Kalluk reminisces about a place, about a hundred miles to the east, where he's been going to hunt walrus. He has known about the spot as long as he can remember; his parents told him about it when he was growing up in distant Pond Inlet. But walrus require stable pack ice to reproduce, and they are growing scarce throughout the region. "There used to be hundreds before—we only catch 10 or less now," he says quietly. "Somehow they have disappeared."

SINKING ISLANDS IN THE PACIFIC

Piers Moore Ede

Rising sea levels are endangering the tiny Pacific island nation of Tuvalu, reports Piers Moore Ede in the following selection. According to the author, the people of Tuvalu have pleaded in vain to world leaders to try to reverse the global warming trend, which they believe could save their home. As ocean waters threatened to engulf the island, Ede relates, the people of Tuvalu were forced to begin relocating to New Zealand in 2002. Tuvalu's plight raises serious questions about how the people of these tiny islands can be compensated for the loss of their entire culture and way of life, Ede notes. Nor is Tuvalu the only island nation at risk, he explains: According to scientific reports, more islands will disappear beneath the waves as global warming continues to produce worldwide climate change. Ede is a freelance writer based in London, England, who has written for publications such as *Earth Island Journal, Traveller*, and *Ecologist*.

Tuvalu is one of the smallest and most remote countries on earth. About halfway between Hawaii and Australia, it is one of the nine tiny atolls in the South Pacific that represent the Oceania island group. They're studded with coconut palms and chalk white beaches. One imagines Robinson Crusoe might have washed up on such a place. Yet tragedy is on the horizon. With predicted sea level increases of up to 88 cm in the next century, the islanders are facing the imminent possibility that Tuvalu may follow Atlantis to a watery grave.

In 1997, at the now-famous Kyoto conference convened to discuss climate change, Tuvalu's Prime Minister Koloa Talake delivered an impassioned speech to the world's leaders, imploring them to act immediately:

> There is an asserted consensus that binding significant targets to reduce greenhouse gases are essential, if the catastrophic impacts of climate change on the livelihood and existence of people are to be limited. . . . For the people of low-lying island states of the world, however, and certainly

Piers Moore Ede, "The Sinking Feeling," *Earth Island Journal*, vol. 17, Winter 2002, pp. 39–40. Copyright © 2002 by the Earth Island Institute. Reproduced by permission.

of my small island country of Tuvalu in the Pacific, this is no longer a debatable argument. The impacts of global warming on our islands are real, and are already threatening our very survival and existence.

Fighting for Survival

Unfortunately, Talake's plea seemed to fall on deaf ears. Neither America or Australia—the two countries with the highest per-capita greenhouse gas emissions—ratified the Kyoto Protocol. . . . Already facing major floods, Tuvalu is preparing itself for repatriation. Starting [in 2002], 75 Tuvaluans will be relocated to New Zealand each year.

The prime minister, meanwhile, has hired law firms in both the US and Australia to help them build a court case against the world's greenhouse polluters. He plans to take the case to the International Court of Justice (ICJ) in The Hague. Australian legal experts have warned their government to take the suit seriously, especially since it accepts the judgement of the International Court of Justice without reservation. Whatever the outcome, the court case will certainly attract worldwide media attention.

For now, life is relatively peaceful for Tuvalu's 11,000 inhabitants. Subsistence agriculture and fishing still form the basis of the country's economy, though in recent years the sale of territorial shipping rights to the international fisheries has pumped much needed money into the country. But the locals are very aware of what may be in store for them. As one of the most isolated nations on earth, the sea plays an integral role in their lives. They maintain a healthy respect for it. The fishermen have been among the first to notice the everyday effects of climate change. Many of the big islands that surround Tuvalu have shrunk to less than half their original size.

It will most probably not be complete inundation, however, that spells disaster for Tuvalu. Before the island is completely submerged, increasingly frequent storms will simply make life impossible on the island. Higher tides will increase the salinity of the soil to such an extent that the Tuvaluans' traditional crops such as pulaka will be unable to survive.

Questions About the Future

Looming repatriation has cast a gloomy shadow over this tranquil place. Those who are not already planning migration cannot help but consider it as, one by one, their friends and neighbors desert the sinking ship. Yet despite New Zealand's warm welcome, some islanders hold serious reservations about the quality of life in an industrialized country.

Equally serious questions are raised about Tuvalu's economic future once people have left. Will they still retain the rights to the territorial waters? Can they ever be compensated for the loss of their entire culture beneath the waves and, if so, at whose feet can the bill be laid? Andrews Sims, a leading expert in the field of "ecological debt," suggests that such questions will become more and more pertinent as the long-term crises provoked by richer countries come to fruition. "Ecological debt, where the rich take up more than their share of a finite environmental space, gives developing countries the moral high ground in international negotiations. There should be no question now of poor countries giving one cent of unpayable debt service to any rich country creditor before ecological debts are reconciled."

Australia responded . . . to criticisms of its environmental stance with a report from its National Tidal Facility (NTF), which declared there to be "no visible evidence of an acceleration in sea level trends." Instead, Bill Mitchell of the NTF suggested the islanders themselves were responsible for the flooding due to cutting down too many coconut palms, population density, and poor environmental management.

Tuvalu has responded with derision to Australia's rebuff, pointing to statistics from the Intergovernmental Panel on Climate Change (IPCC). An independent Greenpeace report also predicts a palpable sea rise, concluding Tuvalu and Kiribati to be "the most vulnerable countries."

Conflict Between Neighbors

Feelings between the two nations have worsened further still, . . . after Australia's refusal to grant Tuvaluans any immigration rights. In conversation with the BBC, Paani Laupepa, Tuvalu's Assistant Secretary of Natural Resources, Energy and Environment, said "While New Zealand responded positively in the true Pacific way of helping one's neighbors, Australia on the other hand has slammed the door in our face."

Australia, perhaps wishing to hammer its stance home, has since asked Tuvalu to shelter Middle Eastern asylum seekers on their own turf. Since August 2001, Australia has turned away almost 2000 asylum seekers, referring them to the smaller Pacific nations to have their claims processed. Tuvalu government spokesman Panapa Nelesone has said: "We ask them for space and now they're sending us their own people."

The forecast looks bad indeed for Tuvalu. Other island and coastal nations will be next. Though polluters are doing their best to look the other way, the evidence is already overpowering that catastrophic climate change is on its way. The 1990s was the hottest decade ever recorded, glaciers at both poles are in retreat, and Kilimanjaro's snows are receding. Without caps on greenhouse emissions, the myth of Atlantis may soon become a reality.

CHAPTER 3

SOLVING THE GLOBAL
WARMING PROBLEM

Contemporary Issues
Companion

THE INTERNATIONAL COMMUNITY MUST ACT TOGETHER TO SOLVE GLOBAL WARMING

Seth Dunn

In the following selection, Worldwatch Institute research associate Seth Dunn assesses the effectiveness of international policies designed to curtail climate change. Many nations, both industrialized and developing, are implementing various policies intended to reduce greenhouse gas emissions, Dunn writes. However, he argues, it is crucial for the international community to coordinate these efforts and develop a consistent worldwide action plan to curb global warming. According to the author, some industrialized nations—particularly large greenhouse gas emitters such as the United States, Canada, and Australia—have resisted taking a leadership role, making it difficult to foster international cooperation in the implementation of effective global warming policies. The world's nations must achieve consensus on global warming policy, he asserts, if the threat of catastrophic climate change is to be reversed. Dunn is the author of *Reading the Weathervane: Climate Policy from Rio to Johannesburg.*

Just a few of the leading emitters of greenhouse gases—the United Kingdom, Germany, and Russia—have met their Rio de Janeiro Convention on Climate Change targets and are on course to meet their Kyoto Protocol goals. Nevertheless, most governments of industrial nations are stepping up their activity in the area of climate policy. Indeed, the International Energy Agency (IEA) has identified more than 300 separate measures that its members undertook during 1999 to address climate change. The IEA placed these actions in five general categories: fiscal policy, market policy, regulatory policy, research and development (R&D) policy, and policy processes, and noted that "good practice" climate policies should maximize economic efficiency and environmental protection, be politically feasible, minimize red tape and overhead, and have positive effects on other areas, such as competition, trade, and social welfare.

Seth Dunn, "Seeking Agreement on International Climate Policymaking," *USA Today Magazine*, vol. 131, January 2003, pp. 52–55. Copyright © 2003 by the Society for the Advancement of Education. Reproduced by permission.

While there is no "silver bullet" climate policy that can be applied across all countries, experience suggests that getting the prices right through subsidy reform and tax policy is crucial. Market approaches and a mix of policies—including voluntary agreements, standards, incentives, and R&D—are needed, too. Important as well are monitoring and assessment, good institutions, and international cooperation. Even if their rationale is strong, however, climate policies run into the formidable barriers of perceived high cost and limited political will to act.

Fiscal Policies

Climate-related fiscal policies have become increasingly popular, with nearly all industrial nations adopting such measures, although most are modest in size. These are appealing because they tend to reduce greenhouse gas emissions while stimulating national economies. A good example is the phase-down of coal subsidies in Belgium, Japan, Portugal, and the United Kingdom from more than $13,000,000,000 in 1990 to less than $7,000,000,000 by the end of the decade. Subsidies are being added to promote more-efficient vehicles and renewable energy in power generation, the most-successful example being the German electricity feed law, which has spurred the wind power business and been replicated in several other European countries.

Nineteen industrial nations are planning more than 60 tax policy changes that will affect emissions, although just 11 of these are defined as carbon or emissions taxes. The most-effective carbon taxes to date are found in Scandinavia. Norway's levy, for instance, was adopted in 1991 and has reportedly lowered carbon emissions from power plants by 21%. One reason such taxes have been adopted slowly or contain exemptions is that their impact on fairness and competitiveness is often overstated by industry.

Interest in market-based mechanisms has also risen, due to their expected cost-effectiveness and the success of the U.S. sulfur emissions trading program, which has helped to reduce such emissions by 24% since the program was instituted in 1990. Several countries, along with the European Union (EU), have adopted greenhouse gas emissions trading proposals, and a growing number are considering their adoption. A Pew Center study on global climate change reported that emissions trading is becoming a "policy of choice" for addressing the issue. An international greenhouse gas market is emerging—an estimated 85–105,000,000 tons of carbon dioxide (CO_2) equivalent have been traded since 1996, nearly half of this in 2001 alone—but in the absence of an international agreement, it is evolving in fragmented fashion. For instance, the British, Danish, and EU systems vary considerably in approach, and it will be necessary to reconcile them into a global framework if the trading is to be as economically and environmentally effective as possible.

The third discernible area of growing activity is voluntary agreements, which arise from negotiations between government and business or industry associations. These are attractive because they arouse less political resistance from industry than coercive measures, require little overhead, and can be complemented by fiscal and regulatory measures. Twenty-one voluntary agreements were initiated in 1999 by industrial nations, including four for power generation, two for transport, and 11 for industry and manufacturing. With respect to stringency, they are characterized by the IEA as "strong" (in the Netherlands), containing legally binding objectives and the threat of regulation for noncompliance; "weak" (in Canada), lacking penalties for noncompliance, but having incentives for achieving the targets; or "cooperative" (in U.S. manufacturing), with incentives for developing and implementing new technology, but lacking specific targets.

While voluntary agreements are relatively new, some interesting results already have emerged. The German and Japanese business communities have made substantial progress in meeting efficiency targets. Also worth mentioning are the Netherlands' long-term agreements with energy-intensive industry, which achieved a 20% energy efficiency improvement between 1989 and 2000. The United Nations Energy Programme (UNEP) and the World Energy Council (WEC) have identified more than 700 voluntary projects to cut back greenhouse gas emissions that are just completed, under way, or planned by industry. These have achieved a reduction of 1,300,000,000 tons of CO_2 equivalent, and a 2,000,000,000-ton target has been set for 2010. However, UNEP and WEC believe that, even as industry activity grows, governments remain too reactive—suggesting that industry could, given the right framework, move much faster than is encouraged by current government arrangements.

While these studies indicate a growing engagement by industrial nation governments in dealing with climate change, the IEA observes that "there remains considerable scope for further improvements." It concludes that policies already enacted and proposed may not suffice for countries to meet their Kyoto targets, and that further action may be necessary.

Evaluating Climate Policy

In addition to identifying good practices, it is critical, in evaluating climate policy over the past decade, to compare governments' broader approaches with those recommended by the International Panel on Climate Change (IPCC). We need to ask: Did countries take a "portfolio" approach to climate policy, emphasizing a mix of instruments? Did they integrate policies with the non-climate objectives of other social and economic policies? Did they account for the ancillary benefits of policies that cut emissions? Did they coordinate actions internationally? Did they follow the principle that earlier action provides greater flexibility in moving toward long-term goals? Applying these yardsticks to the country studies shows that:

- Efforts to develop a "balanced, diversified portfolio" of policies are incomplete, with many governments relying mainly on [one type] of measure.
- Integration of climate change with the non-climate objectives of other policies has been highly limited.
- There has been little effort to assess the ancillary benefits of policies that reduce emissions.
- Few actions have been coordinated internationally.
- An emphasis on the importance of early action is not evident.

Why have countries largely failed to follow these IPCC recommendations? There are many reasons that partly explain this divergence between the theory and practice of climate policy. Climate policymaking is still immature, and the varying quality and quantity of information provided by governments—on the policies developed, their level of implementation, and the actual and projected impacts on emissions—make it difficult to assess what is being attempted, much less what is really being done, and what the impact has been. Therefore, continued progress in the reporting and review of national climate policy is needed. In particular, a more-rigorous accounting of the specific emissions impacts of individual policies is required to assess which policies are most effective and to enable the broader replication of the good practices that do exist.

Variance in the Degree of Commitment

To the extent that one can accurately compare the climate policies of different countries, it is evident that some are measuring up better than others. The degree of commitment to the climate change issue ranges widely among governments, for several reasons. In some countries, public awareness of the seriousness of the issue is strong, while in others, there is still just a vague understanding. In some countries, the issue has broad political support; in others, it divides sharply along party lines. These cultural factors help explain why, for example, the United Kingdom, German, and Japanese policies are clearly more integrated than those of Australia, Canada, and the U.S. Equally evident is that all could be doing much better with respect to each of the climate policy benchmarks.

It has been proved that effective climate policymaking can be weakened by the misuse of projections. In the case of the U.S., overly optimistic projections of business-as-usual emissions trends—based on unrealistic assumptions about economic growth and energy prices—led to the development of inadequate policies. A number of them were partially implemented or discontinued, resulting in even-lower emissions cuts than expected. This combination of events caused U.S. emissions to balloon over the past decade. In the future, governments must resist the temptation to misrepresent the future in order to justify present climate policy.

It has been seen as well that climate-related policies can be overwhelmed by often longstanding "perverse practices" in the energy and transport sectors. Fossil fuel subsidies in many nations keep the cost of these fuels artificially low and continue to inhibit greatly more climate-friendly patterns of energy use. It is hardly surprising that the countries struggling most with emissions—the U.S., Canada, and Australia—exemplify the frontier mentality vis-a-vis climate policy, continuing to distort prices for fossil fuels as if they and the atmosphere's absorptive capacity for carbon were limitless. By contrast, even limited efforts toward subsidy removal and carbon taxation in Europe have yielded results in reducing emissions.

Also falling into the category of perverse practices are the numerous subsidies for road building, suburban development, and car travel that permeate the developed world—particularly North America, but to an increasing extent Europe as well. The Organisation for Economic Co-operation and Development estimates that removing direct and indirect transport subsidies would reduce sectoral emissions by 10–15%. Indeed, the transport sector has been a major blind spot in climate policy since Rio, receiving very little attention while becoming the fastest-growing source of emissions. This is a political problem, owing to the breadth of issues bearing on transport and industrial resistance to a strengthening of automobile fuel economy standards. It will become increasingly important, as transport is projected to remain the fastest-growing source of emissions through 2020.

Overcoming Obstacles

These perverse practices create a perpetual problem. Those countries formulating new climate policies have failed by and large to acknowledge those policies that undermine efforts to address climate change, much less advocate their reform. Indeed, in just one country report examined in preparing this article—that of Sweden—did we find a section discussing "policies that run counter to the objective of reducing greenhouse gas emissions." For climate policymakers to overcome these obstacles, they must do a better job of recognizing their existence more explicitly and employ economic arguments to overcome political inertia.

Tackling transport, something that industrial nations have yet to do, will be an urgent necessity for developing-nation governments as their climate policies evolve. Transport emissions are projected to grow fastest in the developing world, as these countries continue to experience rapid population growth, urbanization, and increased motorization. Yet, there are a range of policies and strategies—road pricing, public transit investment, and land use planning, for instance—to slow these rates of growth, many of which will alleviate local air pollution, congestion, and road infrastructure expenditures. This will require learning from the experiences—and mistakes—of the industrialized world in their transportation investments.

Another obstacle to better climate policy has been the reluctance in some quarters to acknowledge the climate-related efforts of developing nations. One of the enduring myths of Kyoto, perpetuated largely by opponents of the Protocol in the U.S., is that developing nations would be exempt from any commitments because they lacked the same binding targets. What the case studies suggest, on the contrary, is that, even before such targets are set for them, developing nations are moving to address their emissions—more, some have argued, than many industrial ones. In a 1999 report for the UN Development Programme, Jose Goldemberg and Walter Reid asserted that "clearly, developing countries are not passive spectators in the arena of climate change. They have already taken significant steps to reduce their emissions of greenhouse gases below the levels that would otherwise occur." These countries' experiences demonstrate that many steps to reduce emissions make sense on economic grounds alone—a lesson that could be usefully exported from south to north.

The Need for a Global Framework

Among the many impediments to effective climate policymaking in industrial and developing nations alike, the one looming largest has been the absence of leadership among industrial nations to agree to binding, specific commitments to reduce emissions. Indeed, the evidence makes it abundantly clear that the purely voluntary approach of the Rio treaty failed to promote strong domestic climate policymaking over the past decade and was therefore not up to the job of promoting meaningful progress toward reducing global carbon emissions. This conclusion, in turn, points to the vital importance of a global—and binding—framework to coordinate and accelerate action on climate change.

Increasingly, the need to coordinate climate policy globally has been accepted and advocated by distinguished economists. Joseph Stiglitz of Columbia University argues in a 2001 paper—released the day after he won the Nobel Prize in economics—that significant movement on climate change requires that governments move on two fronts: to adopt cost-effective domestic climate policies and to set an "agenda for global collective action." William Nordhaus of Yale University, who has criticized the Kyoto Protocol as being potentially expensive, nonetheless concedes in the November 2001 issue of *Science* that the treaty's mechanisms will "provide valuable insights on how complicated international environmental programs will work. . . . It is hard to see why the United States should not join with other countries in paying for this knowledge."

Reengaging the world's largest emitter in the Kyoto process will be difficult, but essential. Richard Schmalensee, dean of MIT's Sloan School of Management, writes that "the longer the United States, other industrialized nations, and the developing world head down different policy tracks on global warming, the harder it will be to achieve the coordination necessary for effective action." The purely voluntary approach of the [George W.] Bush Administration seems unlikely to change in the near future, notwithstanding the fact that such an approach, which was already questionable under Pres. George H.W. Bush during the 1992 Rio talks, is far less defensible today, with a decade of policy history under our belts. Indeed, we can now confidently discard the claim made in 1992—and recycled today—that soft, voluntary aims would get us where we need to go. To continue to make this case demonstrates either policy amnesia or willful neglect of the record of the past 10 years.

Problems with the U.S. Strategy

U.S. climate policy places political expediency over economics in ignoring the recent success of its sulfur emissions trading experience. This program set a goal of reducing sulfur dioxide (SO_2) emissions by 10,000,000 tons below the 1980 level, tightening restrictions in two phases. In 1995, the first year of compliance, the program cut such emissions 40% below the level required by law. Since then, SO_2 emissions have been decreasing steadily, as has the cost of the reductions. To date, the program's cost has been one-fifth to one-tenth of the $15,000,000,000 estimate made in 1990 by Congress and the Environmental Protection Agency.

In its 2002 Economic Report of the President, the Council of Economic Advisors (CEA) notes that the sulfur emissions trading program "has lowered emissions substantially while yielding considerable cost savings, especially compared with the previous, command-and-control regime." It adds that, "as low-cost options for emission reduction emerged that had not been foreseen in 1989, there has been over time a clear downward trend in the predicted cost of the program." Yet, the report is surprisingly skeptical about applying these lessons to climate policy, calling an international greenhouse gas trading system "impractical" and arguing that "a flexible international program would be unprecedented." Ironically, CEA chair R. Glenn Hubbard had proposed, unsuccessfully, the inclusion of mandatory emissions caps and tradable permits in the Administration's climate policy. At the moment, Hubbard is limited to advocating abstractly the use of "flexible institutions" to deal with climate change, even as such institutions are being built overseas.

Conventional arguments against the Kyoto Protocol—that it would be too costly and excludes developing nations—are belied by American experience in addressing another global environmental problem. It was under the Reagan Administration that the U.S. signed and ratified the 1985 Vienna Convention and 1987 Montreal Protocol to address ozone-layer depletion. As Edward Parson of Harvard University's Kennedy School of Government points out, the first round of the Montreal Protocol did not include binding commitments from China, India, and other developing nations. These commitments were phased in during subsequent amendments, and, since 1987, the Montreal Protocol has achieved a 90% reduction in the use of ozone-depleting chlorofluorocarbons, and at a modest cost.

Finally, the common assumption that U.S. businesses will benefit from their government's unwillingness to ratify the Kyoto Protocol deserves closer examination. In the near term, there may be some advantages over foreign competitors subject to constraints. Over the long term, however, the ongoing policy uncertainty may have an adverse impact, particularly if other countries' climate policies spur technological innovation, open up new markets, and create a global trading system in which U.S. firms are unable to participate.

Converging Strategies

There are ways in which separate U.S. and international strategies might eventually converge. Various proposals for a U.S. national cap-and-trade program for carbon are being considered within the Bush Administration and Congress. One of these proposals, from Richard Morgenstern of Resources for the Future, would combine elements of a tax and trading system to allay concerns that carbon prices may skyrocket. Meanwhile, legal amendments to the Protocol could allow the permits that result from such a program to be recognized in the Kyoto system, and for Kyoto permits to be recognized in the U.S. system. However, this could create significant complications for multinationals operating within and outside the U.S., and could require agreement to certain terms dictated by governments that are already party to the Protocol, just as countries seeking to join the World Trade Organization must demonstrate an adherence to certain internationally accepted norms.

These challenges, and the failure of the U.S. to provide a credible alternative to Kyoto, lend weight to the argument of British climate policy expert Michael Grubb that the Kyoto Protocol remains the best method to achieve global action on climate change. Grubb contends that, if the EU leads an international effort, joining with Japan and Russia, to bring the Protocol into force, the U.S. will be under greater pressure to rejoin. This also would, he concludes, provide a long-term structure for controlling emissions and strengthen the international framework for continuing action. Further, it would demonstrate industrial-country leadership, making it easier to bring other nations on board at a later date, and it would bring to the private sector the certainty it seeks—and needs—regarding regulations and targets in order to foster the technological development and spread of energy-efficient and low-carbon technologies.

Indeed, achieving the entry into force of the Kyoto Protocol at the earliest possible date will maximize the options for governments and businesses to map out strategies for meeting the Kyoto targets and for making progress toward the broader goal of climate stabilization. Bringing the Kyoto Protocol into force is the single most-important action needed to strengthen climate policy at both the national and international levels.

International climate policy would benefit as well from a specific long-term goal, on which scientists have yet to agree. In the June 2002 issue of *Science*, Brown University's Brian O'Neill and Princeton University's Michael Oppenheimer propose a carbon dioxide stabilization target of 450 ppmv (parts per million by volume), but note that this option would be foreclosed by further delay in reducing industrial-nation emissions. They thus conclude that the Kyoto accord "provides a first step that may be necessary for avoiding dangerous climate interference."

Achieving Consensus

Although climate policymaking is still young, a decade of hindsight has made at least two things clear: Climate change has established itself on the radar screen of policymakers around the globe, and it will not be going away any time soon. As Thomas Schelling observes in the May/June 2002 issue of *Foreign Affairs*, "The greenhouse gas issues will persist through the entire century and beyond. Even though the developed nations have not succeeded in finding a collaborative way to approach the issue, it is still early. We have been at it for only a decade. But time should not be wasted getting started. Global climate change may become what nuclear arms control was for the past half century. It took more than a decade to develop a concept of arms control. It is not surprising that it is taking that long to find a way to come to consensus on an approach to the greenhouse problem."

Consensus—at least for this stage of the debate, and for most of the world's governments—may be closer than Schelling thinks. We are living in a moment when the need for multilateral action to address emerging global threats is widely accepted by the international community. It required the tragic terrorist attacks of Sept. 11 [2001], to shock the public and policymakers out of complacency and to spur the necessary and long-overdue changes in counterterrorism policy at home and abroad. We need not wait for a disastrous climate surprise— such as a deadly heat wave, particularly destructive storm, or nearly unmanageable tropical disease outbreak—to move us beyond our current state of complacency and toward the many needed reforms. By implementing the Kyoto Protocol, and by working to further raise public awareness of our vulnerability, we can put the world on a more-certain path toward climate stability and set in motion a second decade of climate policy that builds on the lessons of the first, yet is far more successful.

A GLOBAL WARMING SOLUTION IS NOT NECESSARY

Patrick J. Michaels

Patrick J. Michaels is a senior fellow in environmental studies at the Cato Institute and a professor of environmental sciences at the University of Virginia, Charlottesville. In the following selection, Michaels argues that there is no need to spend time and money attempting to stop global warming. Warming is occurring, Michaels concedes, but not on the scale that the media and environmental organizations would have people believe. In reviewing studies on the impact of global warming, Michaels finds that climate change resulting from warmer temperatures is not likely to have a significant impact on the environment or human health and welfare. The author believes that spending time and resources on solutions to global warming is unnecessary and ultimately will drain money away from solving more serious environmental problems.

Ever since June 23, 1988, when NASA astrophysicist James Hansen testified before Congress that there was a "strong cause and effect relationship" between "the current climate and human alteration of the atmosphere," global warming has been the world's premier environmental issue. Concern over it created an international treaty, the Framework Convention on Climate Change, and an international protocol, the Kyoto Protocol, designed to implement the original treaty. Leading up to his run for the presidency, Al Gore had written passionately that it is the number-one issue confronting mankind.

Yet, many converging lines of scientific and economic evidence lead to the inescapable conclusion that global warming is now understood to be a much more gradual, more benign process than originally thought. Further, there is no known way of significantly stopping it. Therefore, it is time to move on to more important global environmental concerns, such as poverty.

There is no doubt that Earth's surface temperature is warmer than it was 100 years ago, but warming per se can be irrelevant. What matters more is how the planet warms. For example, if human-induced

Patrick J. Michaels, "Global Warming Warnings: A Lot of Hot Air," *USA Today Magazine*, January 2001, p. 18. Copyright © 2001 by the Society for the Advancement of Education. Reproduced by permission.

warming were largely confined to the cold air of winter, few would argue that the issue would be of sufficient magnitude to invoke the enormous costs required for futile attempts at remediation. If the warming were largely confined to the heat of summer, though, the effect would be dramatically different, with withered crops and increasing drought becoming the norm in a world wherein growing population continues to pressure a finite food supply.

The same logic applies to precipitation. Most mathematical models for human-induced global warming project an overall increase in precipitation, and this has undoubtedly been observed in U.S. records. Is this necessarily a bad thing? What if the seasonality results in more water available for agriculture, while at the same time slightly increasing flood frequency? The trade-off is obvious: Many people benefit more by cheaper food than are harmed by floods, and the latter can be contained infrastructurally with modest effort over a long time.

In considering the nature of observed climate change—both before and after human activity induced significant modifications of the natural greenhouse effect—I would like to note that those who argue for large, net negative consequences have an uphill fight. As the greenhouse effect has enhanced, individuals in free societies have seen their life expectancies double, their food production quintuple, and wealth spread and democratize far beyond even the most optimistic projections of 100 years ago.

There are two distinct warmings of similar magnitude. The more recent one has occurred over the last three decades or so, while the first occurred from 1910 to 1940, and is evident in most regional analyses as well. In particular, this early warming is accentuated at high latitudes, where current United Nations Intergovernmental Panel on Climate Change (IPCC) records of temperatures are clearly averaging no warmer than they were 70 years ago (a fact which should have been made clear during news reports about the melting of the Arctic ice cap). The ubiquitous nature of the early warming of the 20th century argues against a human cause. That is because human-induced warming, from increases in greenhouse gases, must be accentuated in cold, dry air. Atmospheric temperature responds logarithmically to an increase in a given greenhouse gas—i.e., the amount of heating is greatest for the first increments.

The Science of Warming

Carbon dioxide and water vapor are two very important greenhouse gases (the latter accounts for nearly 95% of Earth's natural greenhouse effect) that behave quite similarly. Over a portion of their absorption spectra, they are hard to tell apart in their heating ability. Consequently, an atmosphere with very little water vapor in it responds dramatically to an increase in either water vapor or carbon dioxide. Cold air contains much less water vapor than warm air. Over the range of commonly observed surface temperatures, from –40 degrees to +40 degrees C, the vapor pressure of water varies by a factor of 1,000. Thus, addition of carbon dioxide to cold air warms that air differentially. Further, the first increments of warming then allow more water vapor to exist (as its vapor pressure increases), resulting in an enhanced warming.

If this is true, the human greenhouse signal should be especially evident in the coldest air of winter that is away from the ocean—i.e., in Siberia and northwestern Canada. The observed temperature trends in the winter half-year in the last half of the 20th century show that the most dramatic warming is indeed taking place in Siberia, where January temperatures have changed from around –40 degrees C to –38 degrees C.

Over the Northern Hemisphere, the ratio of winter-to-summer warming since World War II is more than 2:1. Within the winter in the Northern Hemisphere, as much as 78% of the warming is confined to the very cold air masses of Siberia and northwestern North America. In fact, the colder it is, the more it warms.

Cold air masses that originate in Siberia or northwestern North America are responsible for limiting the growing season in more temperate latitudes when they migrate southward under favorable jet-stream conditions. Consequently, warming their inherent coldness results in longer growing seasons. Research by R.B. Myneni found that satellite data showed the high latitudes "greening up" a week earlier in the 1990s than they did in the 1980s. A study by John Magnuson shows the reflection of this phenomenon in the timing of freeze on lakes and streams. Interestingly, his record also indicates that warming has been occurring for a much longer period than what could have been provoked by human activity.

It is worth noting that the greatest summer warming is in or near the Sahara Desert. This is also the driest location, verifying greenhouse theory. Enhancing the aridity of the Sahara may be about as ecologically consequential as a thunderstorm over the ocean.

Droughts and Floods

The [1996] report of the IPCC was ambiguous concerning changes in rainfall extremes, stating that "Warmer temperatures will lead to a more vigorous hydrological cycle, with prospects for more severe droughts and/or floods in some places and less severe droughts and/or floods in others." There is little doubt that, strictly speaking, this covers every eventuality, allowing one even to blame weather that is more normal than average (i.e., "less severe droughts and/or floods") on global warming. This statement has served as well as cover for the argument that virtually any weather anomaly can be related to global warming, using the scientific authority of the UN. However, what is the history of droughts and floods as the greenhouse effect has changed?

For many decades, the standard measure of drought has been the Palmer Drought Severity Index (PDSI). It is a statistical measure based upon the departure from average moisture conditions for a region—taking into account precipitation, evaporation, temperature, runoff, and soil storage. Note that the index is only a relative measure based upon the averages for a given location. As a result, areas that are normally extremely arid, such as Death Valley, Calif. (average annual rain: 1.89 inches), are not considered in a "drought" unless precipitation is below this already minimal figure.

All of the variables that comprise the PDSI are then statistically normalized. As a result, when the PDSI is one standard deviation below the mean, a location is considered in "moderate drought." Mathematically, this works out to either one-sixth of the nation at a given moment, or one-sixth of the time for a given place. This is clearly a very debatable notion on how to assign drought. It is hard to believe that neither human beings nor natural vegetation are adapted to conditions that occur 17% of the time.

When the PDSI is two standard deviations below its mean, a region is officially in "extreme drought." This should occur about 2.5% of the time, or, at any given time, over 2.5% of the U.S. It is worth noting that this is not a small area, and means that, on the average, some significant portion of the country will be in a drought that is sufficient to merit coverage on the network news.

This, along with abuse of the UN's statement of increased drought frequency, leaves a clear public impression that drought is increasing as a result of global warming. This is simply not the case. There is no increasing trend in the PDSI data.

Intense Rainfall

Stories about "intense rainfall" and floods are similarly easy to conflate with the UN's catchall statement. They have also been distorted in political discourse. On Earth Day, 1995, Vice-Pres. Gore, speaking at George Washington University, said, "Torrential rains have increased in the summer in agricultural regions." He was referring to a then-unpublished paper by climatologist Tom Karl, which found that the percentage of total rainfall falling from two-to-three-inch-per-24-hour storms has increased, with 11% of all the national rain now coming from such storms, as opposed to nine percent 100 years earlier. Average annual rainfall in 1900 was around 31 inches and has risen to 34 inches today. The difference due to these "heavy" rains (two inches of rain in the summer is usually welcome) can easily be calculated at 0.95 inches per year. In other words, more than two-thirds of the increase in national rainfall that has occurred in the last 100 years is from gentle rains.

A more appropriate way to integrate the changes in flooding rainfall would be to examine streamflow in undisturbed catchments, as has been done by U.S. Geological Survey scientist Harry Lins. He found no increase in the frequency of observed flooding, but a decrease in the likelihood of lowest (drought) flow categories. In other words, objective streamflow records show decreased drought with no increase in flooding rains.

No Health Hazard

Finally, it is worth examining the notion that warmer surface temperatures will lead to increased mortality. Even the conservative *Wall Street Journal* has written that "intense heat waves alone are by 2050 likely to result in increases in death by cardiac and respiratory ills of several thousand per year." The UN's IPCC, based upon data from several North American cities, maintained that "The annual number of heat-related deaths would approximately double by 2020 and would increase severalfold by 2050."

Because there is little hope of any Congressional legislation that would dramatically decrease greenhouse emissions, linking mortality and human-induced warming has long been the holy grail of those seeking massive regulation. That is because demonstration of a health hazard can justify specific executive orders in the absence of legislation.

Research shows that the connection between warming and mortality in the U.S. is simply wrong. Plotting mortality vs. "effective temperature" (an index that combines temperature and humidity) yields a result that is typical for almost all northern locations. There is an overall decline in deaths as effective temperature increases, and there are few very hot days in which mortality is considerably above the observed trend.

These "mortality excursions" are assumed by the IPCC to increase with hotter temperatures. In fact, though, the connection between death and heat has been declining for decades. In many cities, heat-related death excursions have literally been engineered into oblivion thanks to air-conditioning. Further evidence that the decline in deaths is infrastructural is given in newer, southern cities, which have no mortality excursions at high effective temperature.

There are now literally dozens of detailed computer simulations of how the Earth's climate will change as the greenhouse effect enhances. With very few exceptions, they produce a warming with a similar mathematical form—a straight line—despite exponential increases in greenhouse gas concentrations. The main reason for this, as cited earlier, is that the temperature response to greenhouse gas changes begins to damp off at higher concentrations. Therefore, an exponential increase in concentrations is required to simply maintain a constant warming.

In 1996, the UN Climate Panel said, "The balance of evidence suggests a discernible human influence on global climate." This statement is a reasonable summary of the fact that surface warming has largely been confined to the winter half-year and, within that period, to the coldest air masses.

The warming that has evolved in the last third of a century indeed has been a straight line, despite exponential increases in greenhouse gas concentrations. Moreover, the typical climate models also have straight-line warmings.

Accordingly, it becomes eminently clear that, unless almost all of the climate models are wrong, we already know how and how much the atmosphere will warm. We can expect a rise in temperature from greenhouse gases averaging about 1.4 degrees C in this century, with around two-thirds (2 degrees) of that warming in the winter and about 1 degrees in the summer. This is not appreciably different from what has occurred over most of our lifetimes, a period in which a majority of people have enjoyed the prospect of later mortality, better nutrition, and increased wealth. Global warming has been a profound irrelevancy to the quality of our lives.

To reiterate, global warming is impossible to stop. Even if every nation on Earth lived up to its commitments under the Kyoto Protocol, the change in mean surface temperature would be a mere 0.07 degrees C by 2050, as calculated by climatologists from the U.S. National Center for Atmospheric Research. The result is enormous expense with no effect on the climate.

There is little doubt that the greatest correlation in global environmental issues is that between poverty and environmental degradation. How ironic that the Kyoto Protocol—an expensive, failed attempt to stop something that isn't even a problem—will result in a worse environment for us all.

CARBON DIOXIDE EMISSIONS MUST BE REDUCED WORLDWIDE

Economist

The *Economist* is a weekly British magazine that focuses on international news and current events. In the following article, the authors suggest that the long-term strategy for solving the global warming problem must include a drastic reduction in the levels of carbon dioxide emissions. According to the authors, while all fossil fuels contribute to the levels of carbon dioxide in the atmosphere, the primary problem is coal—especially in poor countries, which rely on cheap domestic reserves of coal for much of their energy. Wealthier nations should help coal-reliant countries in the transition to a low-carbon energy system, they maintain. If carbon reduction plans start slowly, with international support and a strong emphasis on research into alternative sources of energy, progress toward stabilizing greenhouse gases can be made, the *Economist* concludes.

What would Winston Churchill have done about climate change? Imagine that Britain's visionary wartime leader had been presented with a potential time bomb capable of wreaking global havoc, although not certain to do so. Warding it off would require concerted global action and economic sacrifice on the home front. Would he have done nothing?

Not if you put it that way. After all, Churchill did not dismiss the Nazi threat for lack of conclusive evidence of Hitler's evil intentions. But the answer might be less straightforward if the following provisos had been added: evidence of this problem would remain cloudy for decades; the worst effects might not be felt for a century; but the costs of tackling the problem would start biting immediately. That, in a nutshell, is the dilemma of climate change. It is asking a great deal of politicians to take action on behalf of voters who have not even been born yet.

One reason why uncertainty over climate looks to be with us for a long time is that the oceans, which absorb carbon from the atmosphere, act as a time-delay mechanism. Their massive thermal inertia means that the climate system responds only very slowly to changes in the composition of the atmosphere. Another complication arises from the relationship between carbon dioxide (CO_2), the principal greenhouse gas (GHG), and sulphur dioxide (SO_2), a common pollutant. Efforts to reduce man-made emissions of GHGs by cutting down on fossil-fuel use will reduce emissions of both gases. The reduction in CO_2 will cut warming, but the concurrent SO_2 cut may mask that effect by contributing to the warming.

There are so many such fuzzy factors—ranging from aerosol particles to clouds to cosmic radiation—that we are likely to see disruptions to familiar climate patterns for many years without knowing why they are happening or what to do about them. Tom Wigley, a leading climate scientist and member of the UN's Intergovernmental Panel on Climate Change (IPCC), goes further. He argues in an excellent book published by the Aspen Institute, *US Policies on Climate Change: What Next?*, that whatever policy changes governments pursue, scientific uncertainties will "make it difficult to detect the effects of such changes, probably for many decades."

As evidence, he points to the negligible short- to medium-term difference in temperature resulting from an array of emissions "pathways" on which the world could choose to embark if it decided to tackle climate change. He plots various strategies for reducing GHGs (including the Kyoto one) that will lead in the next century to the stabilisation of atmospheric concentrations of CO_2 at 550 parts per million (ppm). That is roughly double the level which prevailed in pre-industrial times, and is often mooted by climate scientists as a reasonable target. But even by 2040, the temperature differences between the various options will still be tiny—and certainly within the magnitude of natural climatic variance. In short, in another four decades we will probably still not know if we have over- or undershot.

Ignorance Is Not Bliss

However, that does not mean we know nothing. We do know, for a start, that the "greenhouse effect" is real: without the heat-trapping effect of water vapour, CO_2, methane and other naturally occurring GHGs, our planet would be a lifeless 30°C or so colder. Some of these GHG emissions are captured and stored by "sinks", such as the oceans, forests and agricultural land, as part of nature's carbon cycle.

We also know that since the industrial revolution began, mankind's actions have contributed significantly to that greenhouse effect. Atmospheric concentrations of GHGs have risen from around 280ppm two centuries ago to around 370ppm today, thanks chiefly to mankind's use of fossil fuels and, to a lesser degree, to deforestation and other land-use changes. Both surface temperatures and sea levels have been rising for some time.

There are good reasons to think temperatures will continue rising.

The IPCC has estimated a likely range for that increase of 1.4°C–5.8°C over the next century, although the lower end of that range is more likely. Since what matters is not just the absolute temperature level but the rate of change as well, it makes sense to try to slow down the increase.

The worry is that a rapid rise in temperatures would lead to climate changes that could be devastating for many (though not all) parts of the world. Central America, most of Africa, much of south Asia and northern China could all be hit by droughts, storms and floods and otherwise made miserable. Because they are poor and have the misfortune to live near the tropics, those most likely to be affected will be least able to adapt.

The colder parts of the world may benefit from warming, but they too face perils. One is the conceivable collapse of the Atlantic "conveyor belt", a system of currents that gives much of Europe its relatively mild climate; if temperatures climb too high, say scientists, the system may undergo radical changes that damage both Europe and America. That points to the biggest fear: warming may trigger irreversible changes that transform the earth into a largely uninhabitable environment.

Given that possibility, extremely remote though it is, it is no comfort to know that any attempts to stabilise atmospheric concentrations of GHGs at a particular level will take a very long time. Because of the oceans' thermal inertia, explains Mr Wigley, even once atmospheric concentrations of GHGs are stabilised, it will take decades or centuries for the climate to follow suit. And even then the sea level will continue to rise, perhaps for millennia.

A Plan to Deal with Climate Change

This is a vast challenge, and it is worth bearing in mind that mankind's contribution to warming is the only factor that can be controlled. So the sooner we start drawing up a long-term strategy for climate change, the better.

What should such a grand plan look like? First and foremost, it must be global. Since CO_2 lingers in the atmosphere for a century or more, any plan must also extend across several generations.

The plan must recognise, too, that climate change is nothing new: the climate has fluctuated through history, and mankind has adapted to those changes—and must continue doing so. In the rich world, some of the more obvious measures will include building bigger dykes and flood defences. But since the most vulnerable people are those in poor countries, they too have to be helped to adapt to rising seas and unpredictable storms. Infrastructure improvements will be useful, but the best investment will probably be to help the developing world get wealthier.

It is essential to be clear about the plan's long-term objective. A growing chorus of scientists now argues that we need to keep temperatures from rising by much more than 2–3°C in all. That will require the stabilisation of atmospheric concentrations of GHGs. James Edmonds of the University of Maryland points out that because of the long life of CO_2, stabilisation of CO_2 concentrations is not at all the same thing as stabilisation of CO_2 emissions. That, says Mr Edmonds, points to an unavoidable conclusion: "In the very long term, global net CO_2 emissions must eventually peak and gradually decline toward zero, regardless of whether we go for a target of 350ppm or 1,000ppm."

A Low-Carbon World

That is why the long-term objective for climate policy must be a transition to a low-carbon energy system. Such a transition can be very gradual and need not necessarily lead to a world powered only by bicycles and windmills, for two reasons that are often overlooked.

One involves the precise form in which the carbon in the ground is distributed. According to Michael Grubb of the Carbon Trust, a British quasi-governmental body, the long-term problem is coal. In theory, we can burn all of the conventional oil and natural gas in the ground and still meet the most ambitious goals for tackling climate change. If we do that, we must ensure that the far greater amounts of carbon trapped as coal (and unconventional resources like tar sands) never enter the atmosphere.

The snag is that poor countries are likely to continue burning cheap domestic reserves of coal for decades. That suggests the rich world should speed the development and diffusion of "low carbon" technologies using the energy content of coal without releasing its carbon into the atmosphere. This could be far off, so it still makes sense to keep a watchful eye on the soaring carbon emissions from oil and gas.

The other reason, as Mr Edmonds took care to point out, is that it is net emissions of CO_2 that need to peak and decline. That leaves scope for the continued use of fossil fuels as the main source of modern energy if only some magical way can be found to capture and dispose of the associated CO_2. Happily, scientists already have some magic in the works.

One option is the biological "sequestration" of carbon in forests and agricultural land. Another promising idea is capturing and storing CO_2—underground, as a solid or even at the bottom of the ocean. Planting "energy crops" such as switch-grass and using them in conjunction with sequestration techniques could even result in negative net CO_2 emissions, because such plants use carbon from the atmosphere. If sequestration is combined with techniques for stripping the hydrogen out of this hydrocarbon, then coal could even offer a way to sustainable hydrogen energy.

But is anyone going to pay attention to these long-term principles?

After all, over the past couple of years all participants in the Kyoto debate have excelled at producing short-sighted, selfish and disingenuous arguments. And the political rift continues: the EU and Japan pushed ahead with ratification of the Kyoto treaty [in June 2002], whereas President [George W.] Bush reaffirmed his opposition.

However, go back a decade and you will find precisely those principles enshrined in a treaty approved by the elder George Bush and since reaffirmed by his son: the UN Framework Convention on Climate Change (FCCC). This treaty was perhaps the most important outcome of the Rio summit, and it remains the basis for the international climate-policy regime, including Kyoto.

The treaty is global in nature and long-term in perspective. It commits signatories to pursuing "the stabilisation of GHG concentrations in the atmosphere at a level that would prevent dangerous interference with the climate system." Note that the agreement covers GHG concentrations, not merely emissions. In effect, this commits even gas-guzzling America to the goal of declining emissions.

Better than Kyoto

Crucially, the FCCC treaty not only lays down the ends but also specifies the means: any strategy to achieve stabilisation of GHG concentrations, it insists, "must not be disruptive of the global economy". That was the stumbling block for the Kyoto treaty, which is built upon the FCCC agreement: its targets and timetables proved unrealistic.

Any revised Kyoto treaty or follow-up accord (which must include the United States and the big developing countries) should rest on three basic pillars. First, governments everywhere (but especially in Europe) must understand that a reduction in emissions has to start modestly. That is because the capital stock involved in the global energy system is vast and long-lived, so a dash to scrap fossil-fuel production would be hugely expensive. However, as Mr Grubb points out, that pragmatism must be flanked by policies that encourage a switch to low-carbon technologies when replacing existing plants.

Second, governments everywhere (but especially in America) must send a powerful signal that carbon is going out of fashion. The best way to do this is to levy a carbon tax. However, whether it is done through taxes, mandated restrictions on GHG emissions or market mechanisms is less important than that the signal is sent clearly, forcefully and unambiguously. This is where President Bush's mixed signals have done a lot of harm: America's industry, unlike Europe's, has little incentive to invest in low-carbon technology. The irony is that even some coal-fired utilities in America are now clamouring for CO_2 regulation so that they can invest in new plants with confidence.

The third pillar is to promote science and technology. That means encouraging basic climate and energy research, and giving incentives for spreading the results. Rich countries and aid agencies must also find ways to help the poor world adapt to climate change. This is especially important if the world starts off with small cuts in emissions, leaving deeper cuts for later. That, observes Mr Wigley, means that by mid-century "very large investments would have to have been made—and yet the 'return' on these investments would not be visible. Continued investment is going to require more faith in climate science than currently appears to be the case."

Even a visionary like Churchill might have lost heart in the face of all this uncertainty. Nevertheless, there is a glimmer of hope that today's peacetime politicians may rise to the occasion.

Miracles Sometimes Happen

Two decades ago, the world faced a similar dilemma: evidence of a hole in the ozone layer. Some inconclusive signs suggested that it was man-made, caused by the use of chlorofluorocarbons (CFCs). There was the distant threat of disaster, and the knowledge that a concerted global response was required. Industry was reluctant at first, yet with leadership from Britain and America the Montreal Protocol was signed in 1987. That deal has proved surprisingly successful. The manufacture of CFCs is nearly phased out, and there are already signs that the ozone layer is on the way to recovery.

This story holds several lessons for the admittedly far more complex climate problem. First, it is the rich world which has caused the problem and which must lead the way in solving it. Second, the poor world must agree to help, but is right to insist on being given time— as well as money and technology—to help it adjust. Third, industry holds the key: in the ozone-depletion story, it was only after DuPont and ICI broke ranks with the rest of the CFC manufacturers that a deal became possible. On the climate issue, BP and Shell have similarly broken ranks with Big Oil, but the American energy industry— especially the coal sector—remains hostile.

The final lesson is the most important: that the uncertainty surrounding a threat such as climate change is no excuse for inaction. New scientific evidence shows that the threat from ozone depletion had been much deadlier than was thought at the time when the world decided to act. Churchill would surely have approved.

THE USE OF FOSSIL FUELS SHOULD BE CURTAILED

Vanessa Baird

The use of fossil fuels such as oil, gas, and coal increases the amount of carbon dioxide in the earth's atmosphere, which many scientists believe is a major cause of global warming. In the following selection, Vanessa Baird asserts that in order to stop global warming, the world must overcome its addiction to fossil fuels. Baird acknowledges that this solution will not be easy to implement, since four-fifths of the world's energy currently comes from fossil-based fuels. However, she argues, the switch to renewable sources of energy would be much simpler if the rich, industrialized nations were not resisting the change. In the end, Baird maintains, those living in poor and underdeveloped countries will suffer the most if the world continues its dependence on fossil-based energy sources. Baird is the coeditor of *New Internationalist*, a monthly British magazine that focuses on issues of world poverty and inequality.

It was easy. Glued to our screens we saw how easy it was. As the liberators looked on—or looked away, or chose to be elsewhere—looters took lifesaving medical equipment from hospitals. Computers, incubators, heart-monitors.

According to some reports, sick and wounded patients were turned out of their beds so that these could be taken too.

Building after official building received similar treatment in Baghdad's post-invasion chaos. Centuries of human history, the beginnings of civilization as we know it, lay trashed in Iraq's National Museum.

Nothing was safe. Well, almost nothing. US marines did guard two official buildings. One was the Iraqi Ministry of the Interior. The other—the Ministry of Oil.

The choice was eloquent. No further explication of Allied priorities needed here.

The events of [early 2003] should leave us in no doubt about the violence, turmoil and insecurity that accompanies our addiction to fossil fuels.

As the 'great powers' scramble for the spoils—each ostensibly wanting to 'help' the Iraqis rebuild their economy, of course—it looks like more trouble ahead.

The battle for control over the world's energy reserves is on. And with the knowledge that they are not infinite—oil scheduled to peak round about 2015 with significant shortfalls by 2020 as reserves begin to run out—the scramble is likely to get bloodier. . . .

Unless the world wakes up to the fact that we shouldn't be fighting over oil. In fact we probably shouldn't be doing anything over oil apart from leaving the damn stuff where it is. Under the sand or water or rainforest. Along with other fossil fuels like coal and gas.

A nice, but unrealistic, idea, surely? A massive four-fifths of the energy the world uses comes from carbon-based fossil fuels. They form the basis of our industrial economy.

But if climate scientists are right, being realistic is going to involve breaking that carbon lock. We will have to make the big switch to renewable energy and embrace sustainability—and fast.

Why? Because climate change is upon us. [The year 2002] was the second hottest on record, pipped only by 1998. Australia experienced devastating droughts and bushfires. Indonesia saw weeks of incessant rain and the worst flooding in decades. In India, 1,000 people died in a heatwave. Rivers burst their banks and crashed through Germany, Russia and the Czech Republic. As temperatures rose in Antarctica, 3,250 square kilometres of the Larsen B ice shelf collapsed. Scientists found that the global icemelt rate had doubled since 1988 and predicted the sea could rise by 27 centimetres by 2100. But already Native Alaskans were having to leave their rapidly shrinking island village of Shishmaref. On the opposite side of the world the 10,000 citizens of the low-lying Pacific island of Tuvalu were making plans to emigrate.

The writing is on the wall—and the people pointing to it are not just eco-alarmists or sandwich-board prophets delighting in Cassandrine predictions of doom. The Intergovernmental Panel on Climate Change (IPCC) draws contributions from more than 2,000 scientists from around 100 countries. In their Third Assessment Report (2001) they confirmed that global warming is happening faster than they'd thought, upping their estimates from a rise of 0.45 [degrees] C to 0.60 [degrees] C during the 20th century. Early [in 2003], Canadian researcher Nathan Gillet introduced another dimension. He reported that greenhouse gases were not only increasing the earth's temperature, they were also affecting air pressure. This controls the atmosphere's circulation and can alter rainfall, temperature, winds and storminess. It fits with what we have been seeing.

The consensus of the IPCC scientists is that in order to prevent devastating climate shifts, worldwide emissions of carbon dioxide

(CO_2)—the main greenhouse gas—must drop by 60-to-80 per-cent below their 1990 level within the next few decades.

That then, at its simplest, is the solution. How we get there is the tricky bit.

Making the Change

Most climate scientists are agreed that the massive 30 per-cent rise in global CO_2 since 1750 is mainly due to the human activity of burning fossil fuels. The implications for our carbon-based industrial economy are colossal.

Take the US, the greatest CO_2 producer in the world. About a third comes from transport, a third from industrial heating and cooling and a third from generating electricity in fossil-fuel power plants. So changing one sector can't do the job of producing a 60-to-80 per-cent reduction. Change has to be across the board.

At this point it's tempting to exclaim 'It'll never happen!'—and disengage.

But stay the course. Because change is possible. We know it is because it's happening already.

Today, 10 times more electricity is being generated by wind-power than there was a decade ago; seven times more by solar power. Sun and wind power alone have the potential to meet the world's energy needs several times over—not to mention hydrogen, wave power, tidal power, biomass, micro-hydro and others in a growing host of 'green' renewables.

Millions of people around the world are already tapping that potential and becoming part of the energy revolution. . . . Communities and individuals are busy making the future. And making it work—whether they are Californians road-testing new zero-emission hydrogen fuel-cell cars or Solomon Islanders wiring up electricity in their villages for the first time, thanks to solar power.

International Efforts

Efforts on the international stage are, admittedly, more ambiguous. In 1997, under the auspices of the UN, the world got together to try to agree on a mechanism for reducing global CO_2 emissions. The result: the Kyoto Protocol, ratified [in 2002] by 178 countries. The Protocol obliges industrial nations to reduce their CO_2 emissions by 5.2 per cent of their 1990 levels by 2012.

But the Protocol is resisted by the oil lobby and right-wingers who see it as an interference. It's accepted yet despised by many environmentalists who see it as too weak and full of loopholes to do the job of getting anything like the cuts needed. When the US—responsible for a whopping 25 per cent of CO_2 emissions—decided the Protocol would harm the American economy and withdrew from it, many wondered if there were any point in continuing. The decision of another big polluter, Australia, to copy-cat did not help. But other countries did not let the Bush Administration and its oil-company backers kill Kyoto.

A favourite argument of the anti-Kyoto lobby was that 'global warming' is uncertain and not scientifically proven. It's true that climate science is complex and its predictions full of variables. No-one can say for sure what will happen in the future—and scientists as a species are perhaps least inclined to do so. With climate science it's especially hard to predict exactly when something is going to happen.

One of the most confusing—and worrying—factors is what scientists call 'positive feedback'. This isn't as nice as it sounds. It refers to factors that accelerate climate change and raise the possibility of a chain reaction in the climate system that could effectively put the problem beyond human control. For example, warming decreases soil moisture and this increases the frequency of natural fires which then pump (or 'feed back') even more CO_2 into the atmosphere.

So things can quite suddenly get very much worse with little or no warning. 'We are working without a clock—and no-one knows how much time we have left' is how environmental writer Alexander Evans puts it.

But uncertainty is no reason for doing nothing. You could think a) it may never happen b) it's too late so there's no point in doing anything now. But just how tempting inertia and denial are may depend on where you live in the world and how rich or poor you are.

Climate Inequity

Climate change ultimately affects us all. But our capacity to withstand its consequences can come down to economics. If you are poor you are far more likely to live in an ecologically vulnerable region. This is true of both rural and city folk. Poor people tend to have less solid houses which are more likely to be destroyed or submerged by storms or mudslides. And they are unlikely to be insured. If global warming brings drought and crop failure, poor communities may have nothing to fall back on. The situation looks most precarious for Pacific islanders living a near-subsistence existence and now appealing, with limited success, for refuge in New Zealand/Aotearoa and Australia.

This puts a spotlight on the most shameful aspect of climate inequity.

Australia—which seems determined to refuse refugee status to its Pacific neighbours—is a major exporter of fossil fuel in the region. Its CO_2 emissions per capita are roughly 34 times greater than those of Pacific islanders who risk losing their homelands to rising tides.

So while rich, industrialized nations pump obscene quantities of CO_2 into the world's atmosphere, the poor reap the consequences. Just to get a sense of scale—as they sit down to their evening meal on 2 January a US family will already have used, per person, the equivalent fossil fuels that a family in Tanzania will depend on for the whole year.

Even rapidly industrializing countries like China, India, Brazil and Mexico are committing a fraction of the damage done by the richest. No wonder Indian environmentalists get incensed when tut-tutting Europeans tell them they really should be watching their emissions or when North Americans wax worried about all those Chinese getting cars.

Actually, both China and India have recently strengthened their commitment to renewables. India has one of the largest renewable-energy programmes in the world and is the third-largest producer of solar cells. China has made a big shift away from coal towards less damaging natural gas and renewables, leading to a 3.7 per-cent reduction in carbon emissions in 1998. The US, on the other hand, saw its CO_2 emissions rise by three per cent in 2002 and was the only country in the world to have recorded a decline in wind-power generation in the past decade. In addition the US is now producing monstrous Sports Utility Vehicles (People Carriers is the twee British term) which are even less fuel-efficient than the gas guzzlers of the 1980s.

That the rich world is indebted to the poor world for abusing the earth's atmosphere is without question.

But exactly how much do we owe? Andrew Simms of the New Economics Foundation has been adding up. He finds that disasters caused by climate change have risen fivefold in just two decades. In the 1990s such disasters cost the world three times as much as it was owed by the most heavily indebted poor countries. The case for dropping Third World debt is already strong. Add in the costs of climate damage caused by the rich and it becomes morally irresistible.

But the big question remains: how do we tackle climate change in a way that is both fair and feasible?

Many different proposals are being worked upon. One which is gaining wide support comes from the London-based Global Commons Institute and goes by the somewhat cumbersome title of 'Contraction and Convergence'. . . . The model is based on equal rights per person. It allows for an increase in CO_2 in the atmosphere that would peak at 450 parts per million in 2025 (compared with today's 370 ppm) and stabilize at an ecologically safe level by 2100.

Worsening the Problem

While some are trying to find solutions for the mess we are in, others are doing their best to deepen it. The principal culprits are governments without vision—and corporations with dollar signs in their sights. Sometimes it's hard to tell the two apart.

ExxonMobil (Esso) is not a subtle beast. The world's biggest oil company recorded profits of $15 billion and put $8 billion into further oil exploration in 2001. Its investment in renewable energy is— zero. It cannot even match the modest gestures made by BP, Shell or Texaco in that direction.

What it did put a lot of money into was the US presidential campaign. Of the $1.3 million Exxon donated to political parties in the 2000 election cycle, 89 per cent went to the Republicans. The company also put money into think tanks and lobby groups that deny global warming is happening.

Exxon gets a big bang for their buck. The US President did his best to derail the Kyoto Protocol and a secret memo shows that Exxon was behind Bush's successful push to get climate scientist Robert Watson ousted from the chair of the IPCC.

But most significant of all, ExxonMobil benefits from federal subsidies of about $25 billion a year on fossil fuels—shooting up to $40 billion if you add the defence costs of protecting oil supplies from the Middle East. This is 43 times more public money than has been pledged to clean, renewable technologies.

Exxon is extreme but not alone. The US, too, is extreme but not alone. The pattern is replicated in many parts of the world. British Government gave $10 billion in public money to the nuclear industry [in 2002]. [In 2003], when Prime Minister Tony Blair finally began to honour his election promise to back the green renewable-energy revolution it was with a grant of less than one per cent of that figure and a warning that the industry would have just five years to prove itself or it would be abandoned in favour of . . . nuclear energy.

Getting Real

How about doing it the other way round? One, polluting industries have to pay a tax for their emissions. Two, subsidies are shifted from the old polluters to renewables. Three, some of the subsidies that have been going to the old polluters get redirected to retraining oil, coal, gas and nuclear workers for more secure and long-term jobs in the new, renewable-energy industries.

There is so much governments could be doing to combat global warming. The technology is there. The economics work—or could easily be made to.

But we can't wait for governments to get real—and luckily many people aren't. In the US several states are ignoring Bush and setting their own targets for cutting CO_2 emissions. In Thailand the people have challenged their government's energy plans and are demanding wind and solar power instead. Around the world, in ways practical and political, people are resisting the folly of their leaders.

We have a window of opportunity both to halt global warming and to make the world a fairer place. It may not be open very long. We owe it to ourselves and to future generations to make the best of it.

Or else we leave the world to those who would go to war for oil, again and again. To the lethal junkies at the helm of industry and government who can't kick their fossil habit—and will do their damnedest to make sure that nobody else is given a chance to do so either.

A PROPOSAL FOR INTERNATIONAL FUNDING OF ENERGY ALTERNATIVES

Ross Gelbspan

In the following selection, Ross Gelbspan addresses the need to develop new sources of energy in order to reduce greenhouse gases and curb global warming. Gelbspan notes that several nations and major industrial companies have already begun to implement policies to improve fossil-fuel efficiency, but he argues that ultimately these measures will not do enough to reduce carbon emissions. Instead, he asserts, it is essential to increase the use of renewable energy sources, such as solar power, that do not contribute to the greenhouse effect. Gelbspan proposes establishing a global fund for researching and implementing fossil-fuel alternatives, with the money coming from existing energy subsidies and a modest tax on international currency transactions. Gelbspan is a retired journalist and the author of *The Heat Is On: The Climate Crisis, the Cover-Up, the Prescription.*

The United States is constantly warning against the danger posed by "rogue" states like Iraq or North Korea. But [in] November [2000] we behaved very much like an outlaw nation ourselves by unilaterally scuttling climate talks at The Hague, Netherlands. More than half of the world's industrial nations declared their willingness to cut their consumption of fossil fuels to forestall global warming, but when the United States would commit to nothing more than planting a few trees and buying up cheap pollution allowances from poor countries, the talks collapsed.

The meeting was probably irrelevant anyway. As the three years of frustrating negotiations fell apart, the United Nations–sponsored Intergovernmental Panel on Climate Change (IPCC), which had previously projected an increase in average global temperatures of 3 to 7 degrees Fahrenheit this century, raised its upper estimate to 10.4 degrees. To restabilize the climate, declared the 2,000 eminent climatologists and other scientists, humanity needs to cut its greenhouse-gas emissions ten times more than the 5.2 percent reductions discussed at The Hague.

As heat records continue to be broken and extreme weather events intensify around the world, the reality of global warming is sinking in—everywhere, it seems, except on Capitol Hill. At the 1998 World Economic Forum in Davos, Switzerland, the CEOs of the world's 1,000 biggest corporations surprised organizers by voting climate change the most critical problem facing humanity. European countries are planning drastic reductions in their CO_2 emissions, while growing numbers of corporate leaders are realizing that the necessary transition to highly efficient and renewable energy sources could trigger an unprecedented worldwide economic boom.

This growing international consensus may show us the way to a workable global solution. Instead of The Hague's torturous haggling over the complex minutiae of virtually meaningless goals, the earth's nations could jointly initiate an aggressive worldwide effort to halt and turn back the ominous heating of the globe—and come out stronger, safer, and richer.

Change Is Coming

The alternative is dismal and frightening. A . . . report from the National Climatic Data Center predicts ever harsher droughts, floods, heat waves, and tropical storms as the atmosphere continues to warm. "We found that extreme weather events have had increasing impact on human health, welfare, and finances," said the Center's David Easterling. "This trend is likely to become more intense as the climate continues to change and society becomes more vulnerable to weather and climate extremes."

This vulnerability is underscored by a financial forecast from the world's sixth-largest insurance company. Previous reports from property insurers had emphasized the financial risks to the industry itself, but [in] November [2000] Dr. Andrew Dlugolecki, an executive of the United Kingdom's [largest insurer], CGNU, released a study projecting that infrastructure and other property damage, bank and insurance industry losses, crop failures, and other costs of unchecked climate change could bankrupt the global economy by 2065.

And the coming changes will occur 50 percent faster than previously thought, say researchers at the Hadley Center, the UK's leading climate-research agency. Previous estimates of the rate of climate change have been based on projections of the earth's capacity—at current temperatures—to absorb carbon dioxide through its vegetation and, to a lesser extent, its oceans. For the last 10,000 years, these natural "carbon sinks" have maintained atmospheric carbon levels of about 280 parts per million. Since the late 19th century, however, human use of coal and oil has escalated dramatically, leading to our present atmospheric carbon level of about 360 parts per million—a level not experienced in 420,000 years. In a blow to the United States' hope that planting forests in developing countries could absolve it of the need to conserve energy, Hadley's researchers found that photosynthesis slows as the climate warms. Plants' absorption of CO_2 diminishes, and soils begin to release more carbon than they absorb, turning what had been carbon sinks into carbon sources.

Similarly, a team led by Sydney Levitus, head of the National Oceanic and Atmospheric Administration's Ocean Climate Laboratory, found that while oceans absorb heat, that effect can be temporary. During the 1950s and '60s, the group found, subsurface temperatures in the Atlantic, Pacific, and Indian Oceans rose substantially while atmospheric temperatures remained fairly constant. But in the 1970s atmospheric temperatures trended upward—driven, in part, by warmth released from deep water. "[O]cean heat content may be an early indicator of the warming of surface, air, and sea surface temperatures more than a decade in advance," said Levitus. Later this century, his researchers predicted, the oceans may release even more heat into an already warming atmosphere.

That grim prediction was echoed by a report from the International Geosphere-Biosphere Programme, which cast doubt on the ability of farmland or forests to soak up the vast amounts of CO_2 that humanity is pumping into the atmosphere. "There is no natural 'savior' waiting to assimilate all the anthropogenically produced CO_2 in the coming century," the report concluded.

Downplaying the Crisis

The inadequacy of the percentage goals haggled over at The Hague was underscored by a research team led by Tom M. W. Wigley of the National Center for Atmospheric Research, which estimated that the world must generate about half its power from wind, sun, and other noncarbon sources by the year 2018 to avoid a quadrupling of traditional atmospheric carbon levels, which would almost certainly trigger catastrophic consequences. Writing in the journal *Nature*, Wigley's team recommended "researching, developing, and commercializing carbon-free primary power technologies . . . with the urgency of the Manhattan Project or the Apollo space program."

Far from recognizing that urgency, the United States' official position seems to be to minimize the severity of global warming. This recalcitrance can be traced to a relentless disinformation campaign by the fossil-fuel lobby to dismiss or downplay the climate crisis. For years, coal and oil interests have funded a handful of scientists known as "greenhouse skeptics" who cast doubt on the implications and even existence of global warming. Enormous amounts of money spent by their corporate sponsors have amplified the skeptics' voices out of all proportion to their standing in the scientific community, giving them undue influence on legislators, policymakers, and the media.

But with the skeptics being marginalized by the increasingly united and alarming findings of mainstream science, industry PR campaigns have taken to exaggerating the economic impacts of cutting back on fossil fuels. On the other side are more than 2,500 economists, including 8 Nobel laureates, who proclaimed in a 1997 statement coordinated by the think-tank Redefining Progress that the U.S. economy can weather the change, and even improve productivity in the long run. Industry is also attacking the diplomatic foundations of the Kyoto Protocol—the international agreement The Hague meeting was meant to implement—claiming that the United States would suffer unfairly because developing countries were exempted from the first round of emissions cuts. Yet the rationale for this exemption—that since the industrial nations created the problem, they should be the first to begin to address it—was ratified by President George H.W. Bush himself when he signed the 1992 Rio Treaty.

Carbon Trading Fails to Work

The central mechanism of the Kyoto Protocol, as promoted by the United States, is "emissions trading." That system was intended to find the cheapest way to reduce global carbon levels. It allocated a certain number of carbon emission "credits" to each country, and then permitted nations with greater emissions to buy unused credits from other countries—for example, by financing the planting of trees in Costa Rica.

But international carbon trading turned out to be a shell game. Carbon is burned in far too many places—vehicles, factories, homes, fields—to effectively track even if there were an international monitoring system. Trading also became a huge source of contention between industrial and developing countries. In allocating emission "rights," for instance, all countries were given their 1990 emission levels as a baseline, but the developing nations argue that this would lock in the advantages of the already-industrialized First World. Many developing countries advocate what they claim is a far more democratic, "per capita" basis for allocating emissions, which would grant every American the same quantity of emissions as, say, every resident of India. (Currently, the average American is responsible for about 25 times more CO_2 than the average Indian.)

A second level of inequity embedded in emissions trading is that industrialized countries could buy as many credits from poor countries as they want, banking those big, relatively cheap reductions indefinitely into the future. So when developing countries are eventually obliged to cut their emissions, they will be left with only the most expensive options, such as financing the production of fuel cells or solar installations.

Finally, carbon trading in itself can only go so far; its optimal use would be as a fine-tuning mechanism to help countries achieve the last 10 to 15 percent of their obligations. Measured against what it would take to actually cool the planet, emissions trading is ultimately a form of institutional denial.

Ambitious Goals

Despite U.S. obstructionism, several European countries are now setting more ambitious goals. The United Kingdom [in 2000] committed to reductions of 12.5 percent by 2010, and a royal commission is calling for 60 percent cuts by 2050. Germany is also considering 50 percent cuts. Holland—a country at particular risk from rising sea levels—just completed a plan to slash its emissions by 80 percent in the next 40 years. It will meet those goals through an ambitious program of wind-generated electricity, low-emission vehicles, photovoltaic and solar installations, and other noncarbon energy sources. And a number of developing countries are voluntarily installing solar, wind, and small-scale hydro projects, despite their exemption under the Kyoto Protocol from the first round of cuts.

Some major industrial players are also reading the handwriting on the wall. British Petroleum, despite its attempts to drill in the Arctic National Wildlife Refuge, is investing substantial resources in solar power. The company, which now promotes itself as "Beyond Petroleum," anticipates doing $1 billion a year in solar commerce by the end of the decade. Shell has created a $500 million renewable-energy company. In fact, most of the major oil companies—with the notable exception of ExxonMobil—now acknowledge the reality of climate change. In the automotive arena, Ford and DaimlerChrysler have invested $1 billion in a joint venture to put fuel-cell-powered cars on the market in 2004. And William Clay Ford recently declared "an end to the 100-year reign of the internal combustion engine."

While some environmentalists dismiss these initiatives as "greenwashing," they mark an enormous change in industry's public posture. Only [a few years] ago, working through such groups as the Western Fuels Association and the Global Climate Coalition, the oil and coal companies sought to dismiss the reality of climate change and cast doubt on the findings of the IPCC. Today, with these arguments largely discredited, the Global Climate Coalition has essentially collapsed. Oil and auto executives are beginning to choose a new approach: to position their firms as prominent players in the coming new-energy economy. (This doesn't preclude backsliding. In March [2001], conservatives' complaints persuaded Bush to break a campaign promise to regulate CO_2 emissions from power plants—thus hanging out to dry EPA [Environmental Protection Agency] chief Christie Todd Whitman, who had widely promoted the idea, and Treasury Secretary Paul O'Neill, who has called for a crash program to deal with climate change.)

U.S. labor unions are also facing up to the future, working with environmentalists on an agenda to increase jobs while reducing emissions—witness the . . . call by AFLCIO president John Sweeney and Sierra Club executive director Carl Pope for a "package of worker-friendly domestic carbon-emission reduction measures." Building and maintaining the necessary new energy facilities will take an army of skilled workers, which organized labor can provide.

Despite these encouraging developments, the United States continues to obstruct rather than lead the world in addressing climate change. Former president [Bill] Clinton blamed the media, saying that until the public knows more about the threat there will not be sufficient popular support to address the issue in a meaningful way. George W. Bush and Dick Cheney, oilmen both, are more inclined to protect the petroleum industry's short-term profitability than to promote its inevitable transformation.

A Bundle of New Strategies

Thus, the public debate is still stuck in the ineffective Kyoto framework. So [in 1999], a small group of energy executives, economists, energy-policy specialists, and others (including the author) fashioned a bundle of strategies designed to cut carbon emissions by 70 percent, while at the same time creating a surge of new jobs, especially in developing countries.

At present, the United States spends $20 billion a year to subsidize fossil fuels and another $10 billion to subsidize nuclear power. Globally, subsidies for fossil fuels have been estimated at $300 billion a year. If that money were put behind renewable technologies, oil companies would have the incentive to aggressively develop fuel cells, wind farms, and solar systems. (A portion of those subsidies should be used to retrain coal miners and to construct clean-energy manufacturing plants in poor mining regions.)

The strategy also calls on all nations to replace emissions trading with an equitable fossil-fuel efficiency standard. Every country would commit to improving its energy efficiency by a specified amount—say 5 percent—every year until the global 70 percent reduction is attained. By drawing progressively more energy from noncarbon sources, countries would create the mass markets for renewables that would bring down their prices and make them competitive with coal and oil. This approach would be easy to negotiate and easy to monitor: A nation's progress could be measured simply by calculating the annual change in the ratio of its carbon fuel use to its gross domestic product.

A global energy transition will cost a great deal of money (although not nearly as much as ignoring the problem). Until clean-energy infrastructures take root, providing clean energy to poor countries would cost several hundred billion dollars a year, say researchers at the Tellus Institute, an energy-policy think tank in Boston. A prime source for that funding would be a "Tobin tax" on international currency transactions, named after its developer, Nobel prize–winning economist Dr. James Tobin. Every day, speculators trade $1.5 trillion in the world's currency; a tax of a quarter-penny on the dollar would net about $300 billion a year for projects like wind farms in India, fuel-cell factories in South Africa, solar assemblies in El Salvador, and vast, solar-powered hydrogen farms in the Middle East. Unlike a North-South giveaway, the fund is a transfer of resources from the finance sector—in the form of speculative transaction—to the industrial sector—in the form of productive, wealth-generating investments. Banks would be paid a small percentage fee to administer the fund, partly offsetting their loss of income from the contraction of currency trading. Creation of a fund of this magnitude would follow the kind of thinking that gave rise to the Marshall Plan after World War II. Without that investment, the nations of Europe could be a collection of impoverished, squabbling states instead of the fruitful and prosperous trading partners we have today.

This approach has another precedent, in the Montreal Protocol, the treaty that ended the production of ozone-destroying chemicals. It was successful because the same companies that made the destructive chemicals were able to produce their substitutes. The energy industry can be reconfigured in the same way. Several oil executives have said in private conversations that they can, in an orderly fashion, decarbonize their energy supplies. But they need the governments of the world to regulate the process so that all companies can make the transition simultaneously, without losing market share to competitors.

An Extraordinary Opportunity for Change

The plan would be driven by two engines: The progressive-efficiency standard would create the regulatory drive for all nations to transform their energy diets, and the tax generating $300 billion a year for developing countries would create a vast market for clean-energy technologies. It has been endorsed by a number of national delegations—India, Bangladesh, Germany, Mexico, and Britain, among others. While the plan will require refinement, it is of a scale appropriate to the magnitude of the problem.

Ultimately, the climate crisis provides an extraordinary opportunity to help us calibrate competition and cooperation in the global economy, harnessing the world's technical ingenuity and the power of the market within a regulatory framework that reflects a consensus of the world's citizens. The very act of addressing the crisis would acknowledge that we are living on a finite planet and foster a new ethic of sustainability that would permeate our institutions and policies in ways unimaginable today. It could subordinate our current infatuation with commerce and materialism to a restored connection to our natural home, ending the exploitative relationship between our civilization and the planet that supports it.

Angry nature is holding a gun to our heads. Drought-driven wild-fires [in the] summer [of 2000] consumed 6 million acres in the western United States. [In the] fall [of 2000], the United Kingdom experienced its worst flooding since record-keeping began 273 years ago. In Iceland, Europe's biggest glacier is disintegrating. And the sea ice in the Arctic has thinned by 40 percent in the last 40 years.

We have a very small window of opportunity. The choice is clear. The time is short.

CONTRACTION AND CONVERGENCE: A NEW PLAN TO STOP GLOBAL WARMING

Aubrey Meyer, interviewed by Fred Pearce

Aubrey Meyer is a professional violinist and the director of the Global Commons Institute in London, England. In this selection, he is interviewed by *New Scientist* writer Fred Pearce about "contraction and convergence," his solution for reversing global warming. Meyer's plan calls for reducing yearly global emissions to 0.4 tons of carbon per person. Unlike some other proposals, Meyer's formula takes into account the fact that large industrialized nations produce far more carbon emissions per person than do most developing nations. Under this plan, nations with high rates of carbon production, such as the United States, would have to dramatically decrease emissions, whereas other countries, such as India, would already be below the target level of emissions. According to Meyer, the "contraction and convergence" formula represents a fair and balanced solution to the global warming problem.

With the Kyoto Protocol on the verge of collapse, the search is on for a formula to get us off the hook of global warming. One of the main contenders is a proposal by a professional violinist with no scientific training. Aubrey Meyer has entranced scientists and enraged economists and many environmentalists with his idea, but it is winning high-profile backers, such as China and the European Parliament. He says it embraces science, logic, fairness, even art. Could it yet save the world? Fred Pearce gets to the bottom of it.

Fred Pearce: How did a musician get into the high politics of global warming?

Aubrey Meyer: I had been a practising musician and composer for 20 years. In 1988, I wanted to write a musical about Chico Mendes, the assassinated Brazilian rainforest campaigner. I began to explore rainforest politics and was overwhelmed by a sense of tragedy. I could not understand why anyone would want to murder a butterfly collector.

Aubrey Meyer, interviewed by Fred Pearce, "Calling the Tune," *New Scientist*, vol. 171, July 7, 2001, p. 46. Copyright © 2001 by Reed Elsevier Business Publishing, Ltd. Reproduced by permission.

Soon afterwards I joined the Green Party, where four of us formed the Global Commons Institute [GCI] in London to fight to protect the planet's shared resources—the forests, the atmosphere and so on. We scraped together money from supporters, and I've never stopped since.

Did you have any background in science?

I didn't have any background in maths or science. My only real contact with numeracy until GCI got going was the kind of kinetic numeracy of music, its structure, and the discipline which goes with that.

Contraction and Convergence

You developed the formula called contraction and convergence. What is that?

At the early conferences on fighting climate change I saw this hideous charade being played out in which the politics was divorced from the science. The UN's Intergovernmental Panel on Climate Change [IPCC] said we needed a 60 per cent cut in emissions of greenhouse gases to halt global warming. But the politicians had no plan even to stabilise emissions, let alone cut them. So I did some simple calculations. To do what the IPCC wanted meant reducing global emissions to an average 0.4 tonnes of carbon per person per year. That was the contraction part. It seemed to me that the only politically possible way of achieving that was to work towards national entitlements based on size of population. Today, some nations are emitting 20 times more per head than others. The US, for example, emits 5.2 tonnes per head, Britain 2.6 tonnes, India 0.2 tonnes. This means that India could double its emissions while the US would have to come down by more than 90 per cent. That is the convergence part. Clearly no country is going to be able to make those changes immediately, but the beauty of the system is that it allows them to trade in emissions permits.

Other people, like Anil Agarwal, the Indian environmentalist, had similar ideas at that time. Why did yours stick?

Yes, Anil had got very angry when some leading American environmentalists tried to suggest that India, which has one of the world's lowest per capita emissions, was one of the leading causes of global warming because of its large population. But the case against such crazy views wasn't getting anywhere—we needed a new language. I had become fascinated with the graphics capabilities of computers as I saw them as the visual equivalent of musical communication, a universal language. So at GCI we produced large colour graphics showing how countries could converge towards equal per capita emissions while bringing overall emissions down by 60 per cent. You could argue about the rate of the contraction and convergence, of course—whether it should take 20 or 50 years—but basically we had synthesised the whole problem and the whole solution onto a single graphic. For musicians, mathematicians, scientists, it was, frankly, beautiful. I took 300 of these graphs to a climate meeting and put them outside the conference door. They went in 30 seconds. I think contraction and convergence cuts to the chase. It flushes all the politicians out of their hidey-holes.

A Sense of Fairness

Why did it take a musician rather than scientists to come up with it?

Many scientists have taken to it, but perhaps it needed a musician to produce it. Maybe the idea is not intellectual in the usual scientific sense. It has rules but it is also active, and it embraces creativity. It has harmony, rhythm and form. And it embeds an ethic—of equity and survival. We musicians spend a lot of time on repetition and variation. I kept taking variants of these graphics to UN climate meetings.

But it sounds rather idealistic. It may be a fair carve-up of the atmosphere, but the world doesn't really work fairly, does it?

Initially, fairness was just what we were pushing for. I remember quizzing a woman economist at the World Bank on her cost-benefit analysis of cutting greenhouse gas emissions. I pointed out that small island states like the Maldives would almost certainly disappear under her plan. She said: "What's all the fuss about small island states? They will just be compensated; and we can send lifeboats." She had no sense of the depth of disregard for real people contained in that. But the truth is that the rich are as vulnerable as the poor to climate change. So while the fairness of contraction and convergence is a powerful argument, I personally don't think it is the key. The stronger argument is the purely logical one. It doesn't solve all our problems at a stroke, but it creates the framework in which we can solve them. If people disagree, then the challenge for them is to think of something better.

Stirring Debate

Presumably, the big environmental groups embraced the idea.

Far from it. Many have refused to talk to us or even acknowledge our existence.

How come?

I think they took a judgement at the start of the climate debate that the enormity of what we faced was so devastating that you couldn't spring it on ordinary people all at once. And they didn't want to frighten the politicians with grand strategies. They thought contraction and convergence would do that. Instead, they called for sharp cuts in the emissions of developed countries only. It may have been politically correct, but the approach was random and timid.

Greenpeace, timid?

Yes. They were part of this timid approach. They avoided facing the global dimension of the problem. It was tokenism.

But broadly that was the route taken by the Kyoto Protocol. So the timid approach worked, didn't it?

Well, I'd say that the timid approach is why we are in the mess we are in today. The US has ripped it up.

You have annoyed the economists, too.

They annoyed me. The analysis produced by the mainstream economists suggested that this problem was insoluble; that it was too expensive to save the planet. This is because their work conceals daft and immoral assumptions not only about the expendability of natural resources but also of human beings. Climate change is not an economic problem. It is an organisational problem to do with protecting the real atmosphere, the only one we have. It is not good enough for them to just nod at the scientists and say: "Thank you, now we'll tell you how the world works."

What response do you get from scientists?

They really do make an effort to remain calm and neutral in their judgement. Many see that contraction and convergence tries to mirror that objectivity by attempting to respond directly to what scientists say is the situation. But many identify with us in a moral as well as a logical sense. They are also human beings. They have children and think about the future.

The Political Response

Politically, your ideas have not got far yet. By criticising the Kyoto Protocol, have you played into the hands of its opponents, like President George W. Bush?

Bush acknowledges the problem is real and serious and like everyone else he has to face this. Kyoto is probably better than the chaos that is now on the cards, but the odds for getting this deal are dwindling. Anyway, as I see it, the protocol is Plan A. At best, it will moderate increases in emissions a bit—until 2012. So, regardless of what happens to it, there has to be a Plan B. The real question is whether contraction and convergence follows on from the protocol or picks up the pieces when it falls apart.

Who backs it today?

The European Parliament, China, the nonaligned movement, many African nations, the Red Cross, Britain's Royal Commission on Environmental Pollution and [French prime minister] Jacques Chirac have all said they support the idea in principle. Many economists say they have no real quarrel with it, provided it allows countries to trade their emissions entitlements. If the revenues from trade are spent on renewable energy, it will bring the efficiency gains that the economists are so keen on. And it will allow the poorest countries with the low emissions to sell their spare entitlements for profit.

What about the US government?

Some senators already support it. It is the only practical proposal that does what they've asked for, namely simultaneous emissions controls on all countries. It promotes economic efficiency through emissions trading and enables progressive American firms to get involved and make money. That's certainly what I would tell George W. Bush.

That makes you sound like an arch-capitalist, rather than the communist you have sometimes been labelled. How come the Chinese like it?

False dichotomy. The Chinese came on board, at least tentatively, when they realised I was talking about distributing emissions rights. They liked the idea of equal rights rather than equal restrictions. But this is high politics. The US Energy Department got very interested when I said I was going to Beijing. They said: "You'd better watch your back because you're gonna be watched." I got quite nervous. I'm not a diplomat, I'm just a musician. But the idea is not leftist, or even rightist. The morality you can take or leave, but the logic is inescapable.

But don't developing countries have the right to tell the rich countries that they created the problem and should solve it?

So far, most developing countries have indeed united around that message. That may be morally valid, but it is a disastrous strategy for them as well as for the rich world. The carrot for them in adopting contraction and convergence, apart from saving the climate, is that in return for controlling emissions they could get paid to convert their economies to run without fossil fuels.

So your formula meets the needs of both the US and the developing world?

Yes. It's a framework for the retreat from our dependency on fossil fuels. The way I see it, the world starts a race to get out of carbon rather than a race to get into it.

Organizations to Contact

The editors have compiled the following list of organizations concerned with the issues presented in this book. The descriptions are derived from materials provided by the organizations. All have publications or information available for interested readers. The list was compiled on the date of publication of the present volume; the information provided here may change. Be aware that many organizations take several weeks or longer to respond to inquiries, so allow as much time as possible.

Competitive Enterprise Institute (CEI)
1001 Connecticut Ave. NW, Suite 1250, Washington, DC 20036
(202) 331-1010 • fax: (202) 331-0640
e-mail: info@cei.org • Web site: www.cei.org

CEI encourages the use of private incentives and property rights to protect the environment. It advocates removing governmental barriers in order to establish a system in which the private sector would be responsible for the environment. CEI's publications include the monthly newsletter *Monthly Planet* and numerous reports and articles on environmental issues, including *Ecosocialism: Threat to Liberty Around the World* and *Virtually Extinct.*

Earth Island Institute (EII)
300 Broadway, Suite 28, San Francisco, CA 94133
(415) 788-3666
Web site: www.earthisland.org

The Earth Island Institute, founded in 1982 by environmentalist David Brower, develops projects to counteract threats to the global environment. EII provides organizational support for programs designed for the conservation and restoration of the environment. EII publishes the quarterly magazine *Earth Island Journal*, the online journal *The-Edge*, and the electronic newsletter *IslandWire*, as well as various project newsletters.

The George C. Marshall Institute
1625 K St. NW, Suite 1050, Washington, DC 20006
(202) 296-9655 • fax: (202) 296-9714
e-mail: info@marshall.org • Web site: www.marshall.org

The institute is a research group that provides scientific and technical advice and promotes scientific literacy on matters that have an impact on public policy. It is dedicated to providing policy makers and the public with rigorous, clearly written, and unbiased technical analyses of public policies, including policy on global warming. The institute's publications include *Global Warming Update, The Global Warming Experiment,* and *Global Warming and Ozone Hole Controversies: A Challenge to Scientific Judgment.*

Global Warming International Center (GWIC)
22W381 Seventy-fifth St., Naperville, IL 60565-9245
(630) 910-1551 • fax: (630) 910-1561
Web site: www.globalwarming.net

GWIC is an international body that disseminates information on science and policy concerning global warming. It serves both governmental and nongovernmental organizations as well as industries in more than one hundred countries. The center sponsors unbiased research supporting the understanding of global warming and its mitigation and hosts the annual Global Warming International Conference and Expo. It publishes the quarterly newsletter *World Resource Review.*

The Heritage Foundation
214 Massachusetts Ave. NE, Washington, DC 20002-4999
(202) 546-4400 • fax: (202) 546-8328
e-mail: info@heritage.org • Web site: www.heritage.org

The Heritage Foundation is a conservative think tank that supports free enterprise and limited government in environmental matters. Its publications, such as the quarterly *Policy Review* and the *Heritage Lectures*, include studies on the uncertainty of global warming and the greenhouse effect.

International Society of Tropical Foresters (ISTF)
5400 Grosvenor Ln., Bethesda, MD 20814
(301) 897-8720 • fax: (301) 897-3690
Web site: www.istf-bethesda.org

ISTF is an international organization that strives to develop and promote ecologically sound methods of managing and harvesting the world's tropical forests. The society provides information and technical knowledge about the effects of deforestation on agriculture, forestry, industry, and the environment. ISTF publishes the quarterly newsletter *ISTF News.*

Rainforest Action Network (RAN)
221 Pine St., Suite 500, San Francisco, CA 94104
(415) 398-4404 • fax: (415) 398-2732
e-mail: rainforest@ran.org • Web site: www.ran.org

RAN works to preserve the world's rain forests through activism addressing the logging and importation of tropical timber, cattle ranching in rain forests, and the rights of indigenous rain-forest peoples. It also seeks to educate the public about the environmental effects of tropical hardwood logging. RAN's publications include the monthly bulletin *Action Report* and the semiannual *World Rainforest Report.*

Rainforest Alliance
665 Broadway, Suite 500, New York, NY 10012
(212) 677-1900
Web site: www.rainforest-alliance.org

The alliance is composed of individuals concerned with the conservation of tropical forests. Its members strive to expand awareness of the role the United States plays in the fate of tropical forests and to develop and promote sound alternatives to tropical deforestation. The alliance publishes the bimonthly newsletter *The Canopy.*

Reason Foundation
3415 S. Sepulveda Blvd., Suite 400, Los Angeles, CA 90034-6064
(310) 391-2245 • fax: (310) 391-4395
Web site: www.reason.org

The Reason Foundation is a national public policy research organization. It specializes in a variety of policy areas, including the environment, education, and privatization. The foundation publishes the monthly magazine *Reason;* the books *Global Warming: The Greenhouse, White House, and Poorhouse Effect* and *The Case Against Electric Vehicle Mandates in California;* and policy reports and booklets such as *Q&A About Forests and Global Climate Change.*

Sierra Club
85 Second St., 2nd Fl., San Francisco, CA 94105
(415) 977-5500 • fax: (415) 977-5799
e-mail: information@sierraclub.org • Web site: www.sierraclub.org

The Sierra Club is a grassroots organization that promotes the protection and conservation of natural resources. It publishes the bimonthly magazine *Sierra*, the monthly Sierra Club activist resource *The Planet*, and the pamphlet *10 Things You Can Do to Curb Global Warming*, in addition to numerous books and fact sheets.

Stockholm Environment Institute (SEI)
11 Arlington St., Boston, MA 02116-3411
(617) 266-8090 • fax: (617) 266-8303
e-mail: info@tellus.org • Web site: www.tellus.org

Headquartered in Sweden, with offices throughout the world, SEI is a research institute that operates through an international network. The institute focuses on a variety of environmental issues, including climate change, energy use, and freshwater resources. SEI publishes *SEI: An International Environment Bulletin* four times a year, *Energy Report* two to three times a year, and *Environmental Perspectives* three times a year.

Union of Concerned Scientists (UCS)
2 Brattle Sq., Cambridge, MA 02238-9105
(617) 547-5552 • fax: (617) 864-9405
e-mail: menu@ucsusa.org • Web site: www.ucsusa.org

UCS works to advance responsible public policy in areas where science and technology play a vital role. Its programs focus on safe and renewable energy technologies, transportation reform, arms control, and sustainable agriculture. UCS publications include the quarterly magazine *Catalyst*, reports such as *A Small Price to Pay: U.S. Action to Curb Global Warming Is Feasible and Affordable*, and books such as *Common Sense on Climate Change: Practical Solutions to Global Warming*.

World Resources Institute (WRI)
10 G St. NE, Suite 800, Washington, DC 20002
(202) 729-7600 • fax: (202) 729-7610
e-mail: front@wri.org • Web site: www.wri.org

WRI conducts policy research on global resources and environmental conditions. It publishes books, reports, and papers; holds briefings, seminars, and conferences; and provides the print and broadcast media with new perspectives and background materials on environmental issues. The institute's publications include *Changing Drivers: The Impact of Climate Change on Competitiveness and Value Creation in the Automotive Industry* and *Working 9 to 5 on Climate Change: An Office Guide*.

Worldwatch Institute
1776 Massachusetts Ave. NW, Washington, DC 20036-1904
(202) 452-1999 • fax: (202) 296-7365
e-mail: worldwatch@worldwatch.org • Web site: www.worldwatch.org

Worldwatch is a research organization that analyzes and focuses attention on global problems, including environmental concerns such as global warming and the relationship between trade and the environment. It compiles the annual *State of the World* anthology and publishes the bimonthly magazine *World Watch* and the Worldwatch Paper Series, which includes "Unnatural Disasters" and "The Climate of Hope: New Strategies for Stabilizing the World's Atmosphere."

BIBLIOGRAPHY

Books

Tom Athanasiou — *Dead Heat: Global Justice and Global Warming.* New York: Seven Stories, 2002.

John J. Berger — *Beating the Heat: Why and How We Must Combat Global Warming.* Berkeley, CA: Berkeley Hills, 2000.

Donald A. Brown — *American Heat: Ethical Problems with the United States' Response to Global Warming.* Lanham, MD: Rowman & Littlefield, 2002.

Guy Dauncey — *Stormy Weather: 101 Solutions to Global Climate Change.* Gabriola Island, BC: New Society, 2001.

Lydia Dotto — *Storm Warning: Gambling with the Climate of Our Planet.* Toronto: Doubleday Canada, 2000.

Frances Drake — *Global Warming: The Science of Climate Change.* New York: Oxford University Press, 2000.

Vincent Gray — *The Greenhouse Delusion: A Critique of "Climate Change 2001."* Brentwood, Essex, UK: Multi-Science, 2002.

Joyeeta Gupta — *Our Simmering Planet: What to Do About Global Warming?* New York: Zed, 2001.

Robert Hunter — *Thermageddon: Countdown to 2030.* New York: Arcade, 2003.

Bruce E. Johansen — *The Global Warming Desk Reference.* Westport, CT: Greenwood, 2002.

Horace M. Karling, ed. — *Global Climate Change.* Huntington, NY: Nova Science, 2001.

Jeremy K. Leggett — *The Carbon War: Global Warming and the End of the Oil Era.* New York: Routledge, 2001.

Patrick J. Michaels and Robert C. Balling Jr. — *The Satanic Gases: Clearing the Air About Global Warming.* Washington, DC: Cato Institute, 2000.

Thomas Gale Moore — *In Sickness or in Health: The Kyoto Protocol Versus Global Warming.* Stanford, CA: Hoover Institution on War, Revolution, and Peace, 2000.

Martyn Turner and Brian O'Connell — *The Whole World's Watching: Decarbonizing the Economy and Saving the World.* New York: John Wiley, 2001.

David G. Victor — *The Collapse of the Kyoto Protocol and the Struggle to Slow Global Warming.* Princeton, NJ: Princeton University Press, 2001.

Spencer R. Weart — *The Discovery of Global Warming.* Cambridge, MA: Harvard University Press, 2003.

Periodicals

Wallace S. Broecker — "Glaciers That Speak in Tongues," *Natural History*, October 2001.

Peter Bunyard — "Where Now for the World's Climate?" *Ecologist*, February 2001.

Joseph D'Agnese — "Why Has Our Weather Gone Wild?" *Discover*, June 2000.

Economist — "Hot Potato Revisited," November 8, 2003.

Fred Guterl — "The Truth About Global Warming," *Newsweek International*, July 23, 2001.

James Inhofe — "Global Warming: The Worst of All Environmental Scares," *Human Events*, August 4, 2003.

Bruce E. Johansen and Robert T. Reilly — "Arctic Heat Wave," *Progressive*, October 2001.

Nicola Jones — "Sunblock," *New Scientist*, September 23, 2000.

Dylan Otto Krider — "Global Warming Is Good for You!" *Houston Press*, August 15, 2002.

Fred Krupp — "Global Warming and the USA," *Vital Speeches of the Day*, April 15, 2003.

Christine Laurent — "Beating Global Warming with Nuclear Power?" *UNESCO Courier*, February 2001.

Jon Lebkowsky — "Being Green in 2001," *Whole Earth*, Summer 2001.

David L. Levy — "Business and Climate Change," *Dollars & Sense*, January 2001.

Mark Lynas — "Storm Warning," *Geographical*, July 2000.

Mark Lynas — "Too Hot for Heidi," *Ecologist*, November 2000.

Alexander E. MacDonald — "The Wild Card in the Climate Change Debate," *Issues in Science and Technology*, Summer 2001.

David Malakoff — "Global Warning," *Audubon*, December 2003.

George Marshall and Mark Lynas — "Why We Don't Give a Damn," *New Statesman*, December 1, 2003.

Patrick J. Michaels — "Global Warming Warnings: A Lot of Hot Air," *USA Today Magazine*, January 2001.

Jim Motavalli — "Climate Change Reality Check," *E Magazine*, November/December 2003.

David Nicholson-Lord — "The Drowning of the Earth," *New Statesman*, March 6, 2000.

Sid Perkins — "On Thinning Ice," *Science News*, October 4, 2003.

Paul Rauber — "The Melting Point," *Sierra*, July/August 2003.

Janet Sawin — "Long-Range Forecast," *World Watch*, March/April 2003.

David Schneider — "Greenland or Whiteland?" *American Scientist*, September/October 2003.

Stephen H. Schneider   "Facing Global Warming," *World & I*, June 2001.
and Kristin Kuntz-
Durisetti

Scientific American   "Hot Words," August 2003.

Kevin A. Shapiro   "Too Darn Hot?" *Commentary*, June 2001.

Andrew Simms   "Make the Guilty Pay," *New Statesman*, December 8, 2003.

Time   "How to Prevent a Meltdown," April 26, 2000.

Judy Waytiuk   "Arctic Lords on the Ice Edge," *Americas*, July/August 2002.

Karen Wright   "Watery Grave," *Discover*, October 2003.

INDEX